Understanding Survivors of Abuse

Understanding Survivors of Abuse

Stories of Homeless and Runaway Adolescents

Jane Levine Powers
Family Life Development Center
Cornell University

Barbara Weiss Jaklitsch
Family Life Development Center
Cornell University

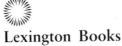

Lexington Books
D.C. Heath and Company/Lexington, Massachusetts/Toronto

Funding for the STAR project was made possible by the United States Department of
Health and Human Services, Office of Human Development Services grant no. 90CJ0090.

Library of Congress Cataloging-in-Publication Data

Powers, Jane Levine
  Understanding survivors of abuse : Stories of adolescent runaways
/ Jane Levine Powers, Barbara Weiss Jaklitsch.
     p.   cm.
  Includes index.
  ISBN 0-669-20902-3 (alk. paper)
  1. Runaway teenagers—United States—Case studies.   2. Homeless
youth—United States—Case studies.   I. Powers, Jane Levine.
II. Title.
HV1431.J35   1989
362.7′4—dc19   89-2475
                                                                 CIP

Published simultaneously in Canada
Printed in the United States of America
International Standard Book Number: 0-669-20902-3
Library of Congress Catalog Card Number: 89-2475

The paper used in this publication meets the minimum requirements of
American National Standard for Information Sciences—Permanence of
Paper for Printed Library Materials, ANSI Z39.48-1984. ∞™

Year and number of this printing:

89 90 91 92 10 9 8 7 6 5 4 3 2 1

Contents

Preface

This book is a product of a federally funded research and demonstration project, Statewide Teamwork for Abused Runaways (STAR), concerned with improving services to maltreated adolescents, particularly runaway and homeless youth. The STAR project involved developing training, coordination, and research strategies in various locations throughout New York State. In our capacities as researchers and trainers, we became frustrated by the lack of information on how maltreatment affects the lives of young people. We realized that the field has little understanding of the many young people who have lived through years of victimization. Although case histories are readily available in the literature and widely used for training, we knew of no source that allowed young people to talk about their lives *in their own words*.

In an attempt to fill this gap, we set out to talk to young adults who, though at one time runaways or homeless, had survived years of abuse and neglect, countless placements in the child welfare system, and life on the streets. Unlike other resources on abuse and neglect or troubled youth, this book takes the somewhat unusual approach of allowing the young people to speak for themselves. These young people's opinions and ideas are rarely solicited: they don't have voting privileges and are typically not involved in decisions that affect their lives, such as their treatment, placement, and education. This is particularly true for those who have been in the child welfare system for many years and are given few opportunities to express their perspective on what is happening to them. As they grow older and move through the child welfare system, their one-on-one contact with caseworkers often decreases as the system increases its reliance upon an ever thickening file.

This book offers a unique opportunity to learn about young people's perspectives on their lives at a point at which kids rarely get a chance to describe their life experiences: the transition from youth to adulthood. These young people describe their lives while their experiences and feelings are still fresh, yet they are old enough to articulate their thoughts in a coherent manner. Currently the child welfare field and the federal government are paying a great deal of attention to preparing young people for independence as they "age out" of care (that is, the foster care system and residential institutions). As a result, a new specialization of care, specific to this age group, is emerging. We will do well to listen to and learn from these stories as these young people engage in preparing for adulthood and independence. We are rediscovering the importance of having estranged adolescents reconnect with their families. We believe that it is valuable for young people to look back over their lives and attempt to understand, resolve, and make sense of what may have been a very difficult and painful childhood.

Method

In order to choose the young people included in this study, we used a two-level screening and selection process whereby we asked staff at runaway and homeless youth programs to consider previous, somewhat older clients (age seventeen to twenty-four) who had a history of maltreatment and who had developed sufficient emotional stability to go through the interview process. We then reviewed anonymous case and screening information, paying particular attention to each youth's emotional maturity and ability to discuss the maltreatment history. Although we have changed *all* identifying information, each youth signed a consent and release form indicating an understanding of the implications of participating in the project. Parental consent was obtained for those under eighteen. A counselor or therapist close to the young person was present at all interviews, not only to ensure the reliability of the information being gathered, but also to provide comfort and support for the young person when needed, particularly if following the interview he or she needed some additional services. Most of the young people needed little encouragement to tell their stories: they were excited by the opportunity to share their experiences with others and found the interview process gratifying.

The two- to three-hour interviews were tape-recorded and later transcribed verbatim. We then edited the transcripts, eliminated the interviewers' questions, resequenced the descriptions of events so that they followed chronologically, and made other minor changes when necessary. Although we interviewed eleven young people, we selected for this book six stories that we believe are representative of the sample. Each story has a unique flavor, reflecting the words, speech patterns, and personality of that young person. The stories document their family backgrounds, their maltreatment histories, coping strategies, resources, and services and agency experiences.

Organization of the Book

This book is divided into two parts: part I presents substantive theoretical and applied information on adolescent maltreatment, including relevant research, definitions, patterns, dynamics, and psychological and behavioral effects. This material provides a background and framework for understanding and interpreting the six stories presented in part II. The last chapter in part I focuses on methods for interviewing maltreated adolescents and is intended for people who work with this population and are mandated to report maltreatment.

Use of the Book

We hope that this book will serve as a tool, demonstrating the effects of maltreatment on the lives of adolescents. Whether used in the classroom or in the field, this book is intended for those who have contact with troubled young people (including child welfare staff, guidance and mental health counselors, foster parents, educators, and family court and law enforcement personnel), to sensitize them to the particular needs, issues, and strengths of this population. We also believe that the book will be of interest and use to policy and legislative planners, and to young people and parents involved in maltreatment.

We have learned that although many young people come to us having suffered generations of family dysfunction, pathology, and, in some cases, poverty, they also come to us with stories of successful struggles for survival. Through a combination of heredity and environmental influences, all the young people with whom we spoke possessed a drive to survive that included self-protective instincts, creative coping strategies, and the ambition to be better than what they came from.

All of the young people with whom we talked have endured years of familial and institutional victimization, life on the streets, and self-destructive behavior. They not only survived, but are now negotiating the tasks of young adulthood by pursuing education, careers, relationships, and independence. Their struggles, resilience, and courage have been an inspiration to us.

Jane Powers
Barbara Jaklitsch

Acknowledgments

We wish to acknowledge and thank the many people who have helped to make this book a reality. First of all, we recognize the very real contribution of the numerous federal officials in the United States Department of Health and Human Services, who funded the STAR project, out of which this book arose. Frank Barry, director of the STAR project, provided support and encouragement in developing and carrying out this effort. Andrea Mooney, Marney Thomas, and Nina Cummings, our colleagues at Cornell's Family Life Development Center, read early drafts of the manuscript and offered critical and useful suggestions. Professors John Doris and John Eckenrode provided overall guidance and leadership for the STAR project. Karen Arnold and Colleen Bushnell quickly and accurately transcribed hundreds of hours of interview tapes; their expert technical assistance was invaluable to the success of this project. Tom Hanna and Madeline Dean provided assistance in connection with the production of the manuscript. Our husbands, Joe Jaklitsch and David Powers, provided endless support and countless hours of child care while we were away from home whether on the road or in the office. We are also grateful to David for his useful editorial comments and suggestions.

This project would not have materialized without the assistance and hard work of the administrators and staff at several runaway and homeless youth programs who recommended and screened appropriate young people, arranged and scheduled interviews, and supported us throughout the interview process. In the interest of preserving the anonymity of the young people interviewed, we will not name these people. We are also grateful to the families who allowed their children to be interviewed. And last, but certainly not least, we want to thank the young people who told us their stories and shared with us their struggles, pain, triumphs, despair, and dreams. Without them this book would never have come about. They hope, as do we, that the stories of their lives can help and inspire all those young people and families whose stories remain untold.

Foreword

Never before has awareness of child abuse, substance abuse, and homelessness been greater. With this recognition has come a growing attention to the plight of runaway and homeless youth, most of whom have experienced all three devastating problems. These youth, forced onto the streets by parents unable or unwilling to care for them, or fleeing abusive, dysfunctional homes, are the children whom everyone—parents, the child welfare system and society, itself—has failed.

The Select Committee on Children, Youth, and Families has documented the impact of years of neglect of our nation's children and families under the past Administration. Nearly 13 million American children are now poor, and millions more live at the edge of poverty; more than 11 million children have no health insurance, while 7 million children fail to receive routine medical care; almost 1.6 million children are abused and neglected each year; and as many as 1.2 million youth run away each year, while at least 500,000 more young children are homeless. Not only is this neglect tragic, but it is costly—to youth and to us as a nation.

Understanding Survivors of Abuse: Stories of Homeless and Runaway Adolescents comes at an opportune time, for there are signs that the tide is changing: corporate leaders, state and federal legislators of both parties, and even the President are replacing skepticism with pragmatism as they acknowledge the wisdom of investing in preventive programs for youth and families. This is good news to runaway youth, who represent the extreme of our failure to provide adequate supports and early intervention services for youth and families at risk.

The early chapters of this book provide an analytical framework which not only elucidates the ensuing poignant stories of the youngsters, but which also will serve to enhance our understanding of adolescent maltreatment and forge improved approaches to treatment.

The following chapters, in which runaway youth candidly share their pain, their anger and fears, and their struggles and triumphs, are particularly compelling. Only these youth can tell what it was actually like to live in a home where abuse and addiction were more common than love and nurturance. Only they can describe what it is actually like to live on the streets, made even more dangerous now with the threats of drug-related violence and AIDS. Only they can say what could have been done to prevent their suffering.

It is my hope that *Understanding Survivors of Abuse* will inspire professionals, advocates, and legislators at every level of government to develop enhanced services for troubled families and youth so that the stories of Jessica, Carrie, Chuck, Elizabeth, Jozeph, and Sasha no longer need to be told.

Congressman George Miller, Chairman
Select Committee on Children, Youth, and Families
U.S. House of Representatives

Prologue

T
he experiences of Carrie, Elizabeth, Chuck, Jozeph, Jessica, and Sasha—the young people you will meet in this book—are not unique, nor do they demonstrate isolated occurrences. Their plight and methods of survival are shared by a host of adolescents and young adults across this country. Everyday, children confronting similar living conditions enter a life on the streets where they are forced to trade their youth, their minds, and their bodies to survive.

The Department of Justice Office of Juvenile Justice and Delinquency Prevention estimates the number of homeless youth to range between 1.4 and 2.4 million. This is a conservative estimate because it is restricted to those youth who have been reported missing or who have had encounters with the legal system. In 1988, the United States Conference of Mayors conducted a survey of major cities to assess the growth in the homeless population. In the twenty-seven cities surveyed, independent youth comprised close to 5 percent of the homeless population. In Denver, Los Angeles, New Orleans, Providence, San Antonio, San Francisco, and San Juan, unaccompanied youth account for at least 10 percent of the homeless population.

In an ideal world, adolescents live with their families until they reach adulthood and are able to venture out on their own. They have had the opportunity to develop interpersonal, educational, and job-training skills which facilitate their independence. Jaklitsch and Powers point out that in the stark realities of the real world, however, this is not always the case. Many young people lack access to a safe, nurturing environment and literally have no alternative to life on the streets. Once there, they are forced into theft and prostitution; they are mentally and physically abused; they suffer from malnutrition and exposure; and, a high percentage of them contract AIDS.

What recourse do they have? Most have no homes to which they can return. Additionally, if they are between the ages of 16 and 21, they are too young to seek refuge in adult shelters and, often, too old for the foster care system. While they are eligible to receive shelter and counseling through the existing network of crisis intervention centers, this assistance is restricted to a two-week period. For those families for which reconciliation is possible, the two-week counseling and mediation period is adequate and practical. For those families in which the relationship with the runaway youth has disintegrated and reunion is not feasible, the two weeks offer a short reprieve from "time on the streets."

Last year, I was joined by Senator Paul Simon (D-IL), a close colleague who has dedicated a great deal of time and energy championing the cause of the impoverished and underrepresented, in amending the Juvenile Justice and Delinquency Prevention Act to incorporate a Homeless Youth Transitional Living Program. As approved by Congress and enacted by the President, this legislation establishes a grant program for community-based projects to expand the services available to runaway and homeless youth. These programs will provide not only the basic necessities such as food and shelter, but counseling, interpersonal skills building, mental and physical health care, education, and job training services as well for up to 540 days. While not a panacea, the grant program offers a more responsive and more realistic array of benefits to those making the transition from adolescence to adulthood without the support of a family unit.

The runaway and homeless youth problem permeates our society. These youths emerge from wealthy suburbs, farm communities, and urban ghettos. *Understanding Survivors of Abuse: Stories of Homeless and Runaway Adolescents* presents poignant case studies of the various struggles, defeats, and occasional triumphs of runaway and homeless youth in this nation. This book should be must reading for those involved in delivering services to this population and for those who develop national policies and programs to alleviate this national tragedy.

Congressman Mickey Leland, Chairman
Select Committee on Hunger
U.S. House of Representatives

Part I
The Issues

1
Maltreatment among Runaway and Homeless Youth

The problems of adolescents leaving home, living on the streets, and being exploited are by no means new. Throughout history, young people have chosen or have been forced into this way of life, and this will continue in the future. Since the late 1960s, however, the problem of runaway and homeless young people in the United States has increased in volume, scope, and visibility. The phenomenon seems to be growing more complex as economic and social forces have contributed to the problems faced by families: financial hardship, substance addiction, and familial homelessness. Each year an estimated 1–1.5 million young people between the ages of ten and seventeen run away from home.[1] The vast majority of them are at high risk for self-destructive behaviors, substance abuse, and physical and mental health problems. On the extreme end, being homeless or on the streets today exposes young people to the lethal risks of AIDS, suicide, murder, and drugs.

Over the past several decades, there has been considerable debate over how to view runaways. Are they delinquents, adventurers, or victims? An early school of thought (from the 1930s until the 1950s) derived mainly from the clinical psychiatric literature portrayed runaways as sick individuals, suffering from deep psychopathological conditions. Relying on the work of Jenkins and his colleagues, the American Psychiatric Society endorsed the "runaway reaction" as a specific mental disorder to be included in their diagnostic manual.[2] Runaway behavior was viewed as a product of deviant personality characteristics, such as impulsivity and lack of inner control. The problem of runaway and homeless youth took on a new significance during the 1960s and 1970s when the number of young people who left home rose dramatically.[3] The psychopathological theories began to be challenged by scholars, such as Brennan and his colleagues, who viewed the problems of youth as stemming from social and familial factors and examined the role of the school, peers, and family as causes or contributing factors to running away.[4] It became clear that in some cases, runaway behavior was an adaptive response to unhealthy, abusive, or deprived living conditions. The "runaway as healthy" perspective viewed runaway behavior in a more positive manner, as a normal developmental process of growth and separation from one's parents.[5]

Those who are familiar with this population and currently work with runaway and homeless adolescents know that these young people are much different from their counterparts of the 1960s who were seeking new life-styles and were rebelling against their parental value system. Many of today's young people are running not to something, but from something, very typically, intolerable home conditions.[6] Increasingly, evidence shows that an alarming percentage of runaway and homeless adolescents in the United States today are on the streets because they have been physically abused, sexually abused, or "pushed out" of their homes by their parents.[7]

There is a growing body of empirical evidence for the link between maltreatment and running away and homelessness. Researchers have demonstrated that a violent home life can lead to runaway behavior.[8] Farber and his colleagues, who found that 75 percent of the 199 runaway young people in their sample had been subjected to severe maltreatment in the year prior to running, concluded that violence in the home significantly contributed to the youths' runaway behavior.[9]

Several studies have shown that in comparison with the general population, runaways exhibit a much higher rate of childhood sexual abuse, including incest.[10] A recent survey reports that on a national level, 61 percent of all runaways have been maltreated.[11] Studies by Lourie and colleagues, Shaffer and Caton, and Nilson all indicate a high incidence of maltreatment among samples of runaways.[12]

Although by leaving home, maltreated young people may remove themselves from harm, they place themselves at risk in other ways. Ill-equipped to survive on their own, homeless adolescents are easily victimized and exploited. During the nineteenth and early twentieth centuries, those who ran away from home had a relatively easy time integrating themselves into the community and securing work roles; in fact, such young people were integral to the growth, discovery, and economic development of the United States.[13] Today's runaway and homeless young people, however, face greater difficulties finding a place for themselves in the economic structure. The current American attitude toward adolescence, which sees it as a moratorium from adult responsibilities, such as work, has destroyed many of the legitimate economic roles into which young people could once fit.[14] In order to survive, increasing numbers of street youth are pushed into prostitution, the drug trade, and other forms of criminal activity. Nearly all juvenile prostitutes were at one time runaways or throwaways.[15]

Young and his colleagues identified other negative consequences of running away. In addition to entering the stigmatizing juvenile justice system, many young people encounter academic and vocational problems because of the interruption of their education; face premature pregnancy and parenting, which can lead to or perpetuate the cycle of poverty; and risk not completing several normal developmental tasks of adolescence.[16]

It is significant, in our view, that the maltreatment of runaways is frequently not recognized, reported, or treated. "Acting out" behaviors, such as criminal activity, prostitution, and drug abuse, bring runaways to the attention of the courts, emergency rooms, and law enforcement and school systems, yet the maltreatment histories of runaways remain hidden, and appropriate services are rarely provided. Many adolescents who are channeled into the juvenile and criminal justice systems are sometimes thrown into adult jails or other facilities that expose them to people involved in more serious criminal behavior. Although federal and state legislation has attempted to address this issue by, for example, instituting policies that separate minors from adult criminals, many young victims continue to be inappropriately served.

The longer adolescents remain on the streets without legitimate employment, the greater the likelihood that they will have trouble with the law and become vulnerable to adults who offer them comfort—for example, prostitutes and pimps.[17] Evidence suggests that chronic runaways eventually become involved with the criminal justice system as offenders and begin to prey on society.[18] Follow-up research shows that chronic runners have higher levels of personal and social dysfunction as young adults, which suggests that professionals should be especially concerned about those who run more than once.[19]

Most of the young people interviewed for this book were chronic runaways, and all had been abused in some way by their families, by other adults, and by the system. Had they received more effective services and intervention when their problems first surfaced their lives might have been easier and less painful. As we read their stories, we can point to various failures of families, educators, social workers, and the child welfare system, and hypothesize in retrospect about what measures might have worked for whom and when.

But somewhere along the line, these young people were positively influenced by individuals: in some cases, relatives; in other cases, teachers who went the extra mile; and in still others, counselors—for example, staff at runaway and homeless youth programs who were particularly effective in helping them. These influential individuals were able to channel the strengths of these young people and to nurture and prepare them for the challenges of adulthood.

2
Adolescent Maltreatment: Definition and Understanding

Not yet adults, and no longer children, adolescents have the needs of both and the status of neither.[1]

The Invisible Victims

Since the discovery of the "battered child syndrome," the problem of child abuse and neglect has been of tremendous concern to researchers, policymakers and service providers.[2] Child abuse has become an accepted, although disturbing, fact of life, an everyday occurrence that has received extensive coverage in both the local and national media. The topic has been extensively researched and discussed in books, articles, and magazines; state and federal legislation has been mandated; intervention and prevention programs have been developed, implemented, and evaluated. The main focus of this attention and concern, however, has been on young children (under the age of twelve), who are believed to be the primary victims of abuse and neglect, and not on adolescents. Thus, it is not surprising that adolescents frequently fall between the "service cracks" in human services agencies and are not a top priority for child welfare workers. It is essential to recognize that many abused children will eventually become abused adolescents.

Defining abuse and neglect, whether it involves children or adolescents, is not an easy task and has caused a great deal of confusion and controversy among scholars and practitioners. Definition is important because it can have a significant effect on the provision of services to maltreated young people and their families: how the problem is defined often determines what services and treatment are offered and received.[3] Are *adolescent abuse* and *child abuse* one and the same phenomenon? If not, how are they different? Does the definition change if the victim is older, and does this hold true for all types of abuse? What about adolescents who were abused as young children? The definition of child abuse and neglect, as outlined in the Child Abuse Prevention and Treatment Act of 1974, applies to all children under the age of eighteen without distinguishing between children and adolescents. Clearly, this is insufficient. In practice, most professionals agree that there are significant differences between child maltreatment and adolescent maltreatment in terms of their identification, etiology, and treatment.

Although the legal definition of child abuse and neglect is broad enough to include adolescents, it may in fact inhibit the identification and understanding of adolescent maltreatment. Adolescent maltreatment is generally thought to be less severe than child maltreatment, and some injuries tend to be overlooked for this reason. For example, the definition of physical abuse focuses on the seriousness of the injury. Adolescents, however, generally do not suffer from the extreme or life-threatening injuries that are often found with younger victims. But whereas physical injuries from abuse are more prevalent and severe among younger children, psychological harm from emotional abuse is more apparent and damaging among teens. Few states, however, have legal definitions of abuse that include standards of emotional abuse and psychological harm appropriate to adolescents.[4]

Society accepts strict, even abusive, disciplining of an adolescent much more readily than it does disciplining of a younger child. There is a great need to differentiate between abuse and discipline. This confusion is further compounded if adolescents are perceived as intentionally contributing to the problem through their acting-out behavior and consequently are considered as deserving the punishment.[5] Clearly, community standards of discipline for adolescents affect definitions and the decision to report.[6]

Another type of adolescent abuse that is frequently not recognized involves those young people who remain in the public child welfare system. Because adolescents are perceived as difficult to work with, and because so many public systems become involved (for example, child welfare, juvenile justice, mental health, and law enforcement agencies), many of these young people tend not to stay in the same placement or facility for very long and instead bounce from placement to placement within and outside of the systems. Such treatment prevents them from receiving adequate services—that is, from forming enduring attachments to other people and from being consistently monitored.

Incidence

Research clearly refutes the myth that young children are the main victims of abuse and neglect and that the risk of maltreatment declines as children grow older. The first National Incidence Study reported that adolescents accounted for 47 percent of the known maltreatment cases, 42 percent of which were substantiated upon investigation.[7] Recent national data from the American Humane Association indicate that 24 percent of the reported cases of child maltreatment involved young people between the ages of twelve and seventeen.[8] Smaller statewide investigations also report a significant percentage of adolescents in official reports of child maltreatment. In Minnesota, Blum and Runyan found that 42.3 percent of all confirmed cases of child maltreatment involved adolescent victims.[9] In a representative sample of official reports of maltreatment drawn from New York State, Powers and Eckenrode found that adolescents represented over one-third of all victims of child maltreatment, and that 46.7 percent of the reports of sexual abuse involving adolescents had a positive determination.[10]

The true prevalence of adolescent maltreatment, however, is even greater than these studies suggest, because abuse and neglect are frequently unrecognized and not reported in this age group.[11] Garbarino and his colleagues have in fact hypothesized that the prevalence of adolescent maltreatment equals or exceeds that of child maltreatment; in their view, our current research is biased against discovering more adolescent victims because samples are usually drawn from settings that are unlikely to identify and service adolescents (for example, hospitals and child protecive services).[12] Indeed, it is common to hear from those trying to help such teens that reports to child protective agencies involving adolescents are given lower priority than reports of similar allegations involving younger children. It may be that adolescents are perceived to be at less risk than younger children because child protective systems are overburdened by enormous caseloads and depleted resources.

Underreporting

Several factors contribute to the failure to recognize, report, and treat abused and neglected adolescents. Actual and perceived differences between children and adolescents influence reporting. Young children are perceived as more vulnerable to physical maltreatment and in greater need of help and protection than are adolescents. They are more vulnerable to the psychological effects of violent treatment because, cognitively, they cannot understand that they are not to blame. Children are defenseless: they cannot speak up and explain what is happening to them; they do not have access to other adults; and they cannot protect themselves, run away, or fight back. They clearly are innocent of any wrongdoing and are not to be blamed.

The perception of adolescents is quite different: they can take care of themselves, run away, and seek help. Unlike the innocent child victim, adolescents suffer from negative stereotyping that tends to promote the perception that young people, because of their erratic and provocative behavior, are often responsible for and deserving of their maltreatment. Although adolescents may be physically as large as adults and, consequently, in less danger of bodily harm, they are still emotionally and psychologically dependent on their parents.[13] This dependency may, in fact, cause them to be submissive to an abusing parent and prevent them from fighting back or seeking intervention.[14] Further, there are risks unique to this age group, such as drug abuse, delinquency, pregnancy, running away, and suicide. These are precisely the sorts of behavior that may mask maltreatment, thereby making identification more difficult. For example, although maltreated young people are frequently brought to the attention of school authorities, police, or probation officers, the maltreatment remains hidden and appropriate services are not provided.[15] The way in which an adolescent enters the services system and the label given to his or her behavior (for example, an "abused" youth or a "delinquent youth") will ultimately determine how that young person is treated and which services he or she receives.[16] This makes the identification of maltreatment among adolescents particularly important for effective treatment and intervention.

Other factors contribute to the failure to notice and serve adolescents. According to Fisher and Berdie, many reported cases of maltreated teens are not accepted by social service agencies because of narrow definitions of abuse and neglect, or because priorities dictate a focus on maltreated younger children.[17] Since adolescents are hard to place and appear uncooperative, child protective agencies sometimes refuse adolescent cases in the hope that the young people will soon reach an age beyond jurisdiction for the state's child protective laws. Often only the most serious, blatant cases of adolescent abuse, mainly sexual abuse, are accepted.

We speculate that although teachers, counselors, and youth workers may recognize maltreatment, they do not always report suspected cases to protective services or the police. Some of them, who may distrust the child welfare system, may want to provide services directly to the individual. Community agencies dealing with abused adolescents, such as runaway and homeless youth programs, may fear that a call to Child Protective Services (CPS) would cause a breach of confidentiality, thereby damaging the trusting relationship that they have established with the youth. This could be detrimental to the agency's or program's reputation in the community, particularly since runaway and homeless youth programs emphasize that they are a "safe place" for kids. Youth workers might fear that social services will not accept, let alone substantiate, the case, since teens are frequently not believed; further, even if the report were accepted, CPS or police intervention would be minimal.

Young people themselves may be reluctant to agree to report. As violence has become a normal part of their lives, they may not perceive themselves as victims of maltreatment. They may feel ashamed and afraid, or want to protect their families. Boys may be particularly reluctant to disclose maltreatment for fear of appearing unmanly, vulnerable, or weak.

When viewed together, many factors influence whether adolescent maltreatment will be disclosed or reported. Consequently, accurate estimates of the incidence of adolescent maltreatment are difficult to obtain.

Working Definitions of Adolescent Abuse and Neglect

Professionals should consider special issues when applying definitions of child abuse and neglect to the identification of maltreatment among adolescents. If maltreated adolescents do not exhibit the clear physical indicators of abuse common in younger children, then agencies may want to develop specific operational definitions for adolescents. The following operational definitions are offered as guidelines toward this end.

Physical Abuse

Physical abuse is considered to have occurred when the adolescent has been nonaccidentally physically harmed in some way, or placed at risk of being physically harmed. Adolescents who are physically maltreated are often not defined as abused because the injuries are not considered sufficiently severe. The physical abuse of teens, because of their age and size, usually does not involve broken bones, spiral fractures, subdural hematomas, or other extreme injuries commonly associated with the physical abuse of infants or younger children. Common indicators of physical abuse among adolescents include bruises, burns, welts, lacerations, or bite marks. Some may sincerely claim that parents or guardians are responsible; others may deny or hide the abuse, claiming, for example, that they were "beat up by some kids." With physical abuse, the older the victim, the greater chance his injury will be seen as both minor and deserved and thus not "abuse."

Neglect

When children of any age are not adequately housed, clothed, or fed, they are being neglected. Many service providers do not think of adolescents as being vulnerable to neglect. However, an alarming number of teens are forced to leave their homes, and consequently, they resort to illegal and dangerous means to support themselves. "Pushouts" or "throwaways" experience a particular type of neglect common among adolescents; these are young people who do not willingly choose to leave home but are forced to leave by their parents with the intention that they not return. Only rarely are "pushouts" reported to CPS as neglected.

The parent who forces an adolescent out of the home prematurely may do so because of financial problems, in order to sustain a romantic relationship, addiction, or because he or she finds the adolescent too difficult to handle. In most states young people are the responsibility of their parents until they are eighteen. If attempts to reunite an adolescent and family have failed because the parents refuse to accept the young person back into the home, there may also be grounds for a neglect report.

Emotional Maltreatment

Emotional maltreatment is usually defined in terms of parental behavior that has a demonstrated negative effect on a child's emotional or psychological development and well-being. This may consist of repeated threats of harm, a persistent lack of concern for a child's welfare, bizarre disciplinary measures, or continual demeaning or degrading of a child.

Emotional maltreatment signifies that the parent or guardian is, or has been, behaving toward the young person in a manner that is causing observable behavioral, academic, or psychological dysfunction. In order for emotional maltreatment to be recognized by the social service or legal system, a cause-and-effect relationship must be demonstrated between the parent's behavior and the youth's dysfunction. Emotional maltreatment could take another form, for example, if a young person is in need of psychological services and the parent is unwilling or unable to assist him or her in obtaining them. In cases in which emotional maltreatment is suspected, a psychological evaluation is frequently required.

According to many service providers who work with maltreated adolescents, emotional maltreatment is one of the most common forms of abuse and neglect, yet it is rarely reported to CPS because it is so difficult to prove and is probably the least visible of all forms of maltreatment. As a basis for intervention, emotional maltreatment is usually insufficient except in extreme circumstances or in conjunction with other types of maltreatment.[18] Some experts believe that emotional maltreatment is really the base for all other types of maltreatment. This form of maltreatment is particularly insidious because there may not be clear actions or behaviors to point to and because the maltreatment may be the sum total of years of verbal or emotional disparagement or psychological sabotage.

Sexual Abuse

Sexual abuse refers to any sexual offense committed, or allowed to be committed, against a young person by a parent or other person legally responsible for him or her. This may include touching a young person for the purpose of sexual gratification or forcing a young person to touch an adult; sexual intercourse; exposing a young person to sexual activity, exhibitionism, or pornography; or permitting a young person to engage in sexual activity that is not developmentally appropriate.

Sexual abuse is a difficult issue, for it is often emotionally laden and until recently its mere mention was considered taboo. Many adults may unconsciously hold beliefs about sexual abuse that make it hard for them to recognize its occurrence. Several facts about sexual abuse have been identified:[19]

The sexual abuser is almost always someone who knows and has access to the young person

There is likely to be a progression of numerous sexual contacts

There are often few, if any, physical or medical signs to corroborate the allegations of abuse

Acts of sexual abuse are usually nonviolent; it is the implied power position of an adult that influences the young person

Initiation, intimidation, stigmatization, isolation, helplessness, and self-blame depend on a terrifying reality of sexual abuse: it occurs only when the young person is alone with the offending adult and must never be shared with anyone else

The young person often has conflicting feelings about the perpetrator and may take steps to protect him or her if there is an accidental disclosure

Mothers (usually the nonabusing parent) typically support their husbands, are disbelieving of the allegations, or, at best, are ambivalent about whom to believe

Without strong support, a young person will normally retract his or her disclosure of abuse[19]

According to Dr. Suzanne Sgroi, the dynamics of sexual abuse usually fall into a predictable pattern.[20] She has identified the following five phases:

1. *Engagement phase.* This phase involves *access* and *opportunity* for a first encounter, including a private place and time; the *relationship of the participants*—the perpetrator is usually someone with frequent access to the young person, such as a family member, relative, or trusted adult; and *inducement*—the perpetrator usually secures the young person's participation by means of low-key, subtle activities. In violent families, force may be a more common means of engagement.

2. *Sexual interaction phase.* During this phase there is usually a progression of sexual activity over time. Although not every case will include the same activities in the same order, most will progress from exposure to fondling to some form of penetration.

3. *Secrecy phase.* In order for the sexual behavior to continue, secrecy must be imposed, and the perpetrator will employ a variety of methods of persuasion and pressure. Most children keep the secret because of the rewards or threats made by the perpetrator; some may have experienced a degree of enjoyment and want the attention or activity to continue. The secret may be preserved for months or years.

4. *Disclosure phase.* Disclosures may be accidental or purposeful. When the disclosure is *accidental,* either through observation by a third party or through the presence of a physical or behavioral indicator, skilled crisis intervention needs to follow. This may include diffusing anger and anxiety, reinforcing the fact that the abuse does exist, establishing the facts, and assisting and initiating intervention planning. When the disclosure is *purposeful*—that is to say, revealed by the young person or participant—the intervention can be planned and coordinated in a more relaxed manner. There may be a wide variety of reactions by alleged perpetrators and nonoffending parents to a disclosure. Out of fear or embarrassment, many will deny the need for assistance and want to handle matters without the involvement of outside agencies.

5. *Suppression phase.* After a disclosure, a young person's family may try to suppress the intervention and encourage the young person to retract the original accusation—that is, to claim that the abuse did not occur and to "admit" that the original disclosure was a lie. Retractions are common occurrences in sexual abuse cases. Reluctant families may deny that there are any significant disturbances resulting from the abuse; they may also ostracize, apply verbal pressure, threaten, or undermine the young person's credibility, claiming that he or she is lying, crazy, or both. Any of these reactions, combined with the extreme vulnerability of the victim following a disclosure, may result in a retraction. This is a time when the young person needs the greatest support.

Patterns of Adolescent Maltreatment

In addition to examining the types of adolescent maltreatment, it is also important to understand the time of onset and related family patterns. Abuse and neglect commonly occur in families when there are stresses such as financial problems, unemployment, marital discord, or alcoholism. Although no two abusive families are identical, observers have noted some general patterns of family dynamics that seem to create the potential for adolescent maltreatment to occur. These observations relate primarily to physical abuse, but many of the dynamics are also applicable to emotional maltreatment, neglect, and sexual abuse. Understanding these patterns may help determine how best to assist these young people and their families.

Abuse that Occurred Only when the Child Was Young. The abused child sometimes does not react outwardly until adolescence, when he or she may begin to demonstrate behavioral problems and act out. Parents may be perplexed by this behavior and not see the connection between the earlier abuse and the adolescent's seemingly bizarre actions. This pattern is particularly common with foster and adopted children who may have repressed abuse that took place when they were with their natural parent(s) or in earlier placements.

Abuse that Occurred during the Toddler and Preschool Years, then Recurred in Adolescence. This type of abuse appears to be associated with issues of separation and individuation, processes that occur during both the toddler and adolescent stages of the life course.

Dr. Ira Lourie has identified three patterns of adolescent abuse that will be described in greater detail.[21] Each pattern describes a particular family dynamic as well as the role the abuse plays in the family.

Abuse Continuing from Childhood into Adolescence. This type of abusive family pattern is characterized as follows:

> It begins when the child is between the age of six and eight
>
> The child is described by the parents as difficult or stubborn
>
> The child is seen by the parents as disrespectful and unresponsive to discipline
>
> The parents are disorganized, either through their own inadequacy or through the child's behavior
>
> The parents are overwhelmed by and unable to master life. They perceive their children as standing in the way of their success. Thus, their children are targets for the expression of their own frustration
>
> The family is socially isolated and lacks outside support
>
> The abuse may be ritualized in accordance with some religious belief in which the function of the abuse is not for the purpose of discipline, but to break the young person's will and spirit

Such abuse becomes visible only when it can no longer be tolerated by the young person. Disclosures frequently occur during adolescence, when the young person becomes more independent and autonomous and is willing to take a stand. If he or she has been psychologically injured by the abuse and does not possess strong coping abilities, acting-out or self-destructive behavior can result. Such adolescents frequently enter the justice system, where the abuse may be overlooked and never addressed.

Abuse Resulting from a Quality Change in Behavior toward the Youth. According to Lourie, this pattern emerges in situations in which the process of becoming an adolescent has triggered changes in the quality of the parents' discipline. This pattern is associated with several characteristics:

Corporal punishment (spanking) of child is accepted by the family and community as an appropriate form of discipline

Spankings or slaps become closed-fisted blows, with greater force

Developmental issues play a strong role in increasing the nature and quality of the anger discharged by the parents. For example, the difficulties of adolescence may be less tolerable to a parent experiencing the difficulties of middle age

Physical abuse may replace emotional abuse

The issues of separation and individuation play a strong role in the pattern of conflict

There can be a substantial increase in the incidence of emotional abuse related to separation

In this abusive pattern, rigid and controlling parents become increasingly frustrated by the adolescent's inability to respond to discipline, or by his or her tendency to disrupt order in the family. The parents respond by becoming increasingly rigid until they finally lose control and become abusive. These young people have been so dominated as children that they have never developed sufficient inner controls. As adolescents they begin to test the control situation, and this testing is perceived as out-of-control behavior by their parents. In some families where a high level of physical punishment is acceptable, the parent may never appear out of control, and the victim may recall, "My father straightened me out by beating me up; it was the best thing that ever happened to me."

Abuse that Begins Only when the Child Reaches Adolescence. This pattern manifests itself in the following manner:

There is no abusive behavior prior to adolescence

The parents describe the child as turning from an "angel" into a "monster" around the age of twelve to fourteen

The parents have difficulty recognizing boundaries between the child and themselves

The young person finds adolescence difficult

The young person engages in provocative behavior and shows unstable emotions

The abuse is sporadic and related to specific incidents

In this pattern of abuse, according to Lourie, the parents are actually very child-oriented and have overindulged the young person during his or her childhood. This "spoiling" can be gratifying to both parent and child, but it tends to infantilize the youngster. When the child reaches adolescence, the parents are not prepared to accept his or her need to move beyond the infantile status and grow up. Rather than going through a gradual separation process and leaving the nest in stages, the adolescent may overcompensate by acting out or running away. Parents of such children have difficulty knowing where they end and their child begins, a dynamic known as "blurred boundaries." Such parents tend to answer questions directed at their teenagers. Because of the lack of boundaries between themselves and their children, they are traumatized by the process of normal adolescent separation.

Family Dynamics of Maltreatment

In addition to the patterns of maltreatment, other family dynamics cause and perpetuate abuse and neglect during adolescence. Because maltreatment is so often intergenerational, it may be difficult to distinguish clearly between cause and effect. Nevertheless, all of the family dynamics described next serve as a reminder that the maltreatment is often related to various types and degrees of broader family dysfunction.

A Phase-Developmental Model

Some of Ira Lourie's observations have created a picture of abuse that takes into account the developmental situation of both the child and the parent(s).[22] This model applies mainly to families in which the parents are at or near middle age (thirty-five), as opposed to those in which they are younger. Lourie's phase-specific model of adolescent abuse contrasts the developmental tasks of adolescents (for example, separation, responsibility) with the developmental tasks of the middle-aged parent (for example, reassessment of the life course). The parent of the adolescent frequently faces midlife crises that may conflict with the tasks of adolescent development. This conflict may lead to abusive behaviors in families that previously have not engaged in abuse. According to Lourie,

> Compounding any trouble the parent has in these mid-life tasks is the fact that characteristics of adolescence naturally conflict. Adolescents are planning their lives, not reassessing; they are denying mortality rather than facing death; they are perceived as having boundless energy, in comparison to decreasing energy; they are falling in love, not divorcing; and their change of life is a positive one. Whatever problems parents might have, the lives of their adolescents rub salt in the wounds.[23]

Thus, basic conflicts can easily explode into violent interactions. The model puts the abusive family dynamic into a perspective that emphasizes the developmental issues, rather than posing the problem in terms of perpetrator and victim.

Teen Parents

Many maltreated young people appearing at agencies today are the children of teenage parents. These families are often difficult to work with. In some cases, the children in these families may be at an older age than the adults were when they became parents. Mothers and daughters often engage in rivalry disputes, and parent/child boundaries are often unclear. The maltreatment is frequently intergenerational and accepted as normal. These families often reflect the first two patterns identified by Lourie: *abuse continuing from childhood* and *quality change at adolescence*. The quality change with these younger families may have more to do with the parents' unfinished separation from their families of origin than it does with the adolescent's attempts at separation.

Parentified Youth

Some abused youth take on parental characteristics to such an extreme that they are described as "parentified." These are young people who, over time, have assumed parenting roles within their families and have taken on psychological and emotional responsibilities well beyond their years and maturity. Such responsibilities might range from a twelve-year-old's having to wake up regularly in the middle of the night to feed a crying infant, to her having to take care of her father's sexual needs. These adolescents seem almost frozen in this role. Parentified young people are easy to identify and work with because they meet everyone else's needs.

They are particularly adept at meeting the emotional needs of their parents. They present themselves as quiet, perfect, pseudoadults, "chameleon-like," and not very demanding. The parentified-child syndrome is observed across all types of serious maltreatment, but most often in cases of incest. It should serve as a "red flag," indicating that serious abuse has taken place. Families exhibiting this pattern are extremely enmeshed and are in need of long-term family therapy, as well as protective service intervention.

The Role of Mothers in Cases of Sexual Abuse

Although fathers and stepfathers are usually the perpetrators in cases of sexual abuse, mothers may play an equally important role in the perpetration of abuse. Still, they are given little attention. The role of mothers should be considered both in terms of their treatment needs and their ability to protect the child from possible revictimization.

Sexual abuse is often a family pattern repeated generation after generation. Often the mothers of sexual abuse victims were themselves victims of earlier maltreatment. If the abuse was repressed, these women may have a variety of unresolved dependency issues: they may deny or be ambivalent about their child's allegation of abuse, or they may become angry with the child for threatening their security. These mothers are often physically and psychologically absent from the home.

When sexual abuse is disclosed, services are typically provided for the victim and the male perpetrator. If the mother goes without treatment, however, she may become involved with another perpetrator who will abuse other children in the home. The mother's ability to prevent a recurrence and her need for treatment should therefore receive due attention.

3
Psychological and Behavioral Effects of Maltreatment

Psychological Effects

Maltreatment, exploitation, and homelessness among young people take their heaviest toll on the emotional and psychological development of young victims. Adolescence is a time of intense emotional, mental, and physical development. Through the developmental processes of separation and individuation, adult identities are formed. These processes can be a challenge and a struggle even for someone growing up in a nurturing, nonabusive family. During adolescence young people normally identify with and push away from their parents. Previous or current maltreatment may seriously disrupt the completion of various developmental tasks that allow for a normal process of individuation and separation. Maltreatment is disruptive and further compounds the normal chaos of adolescent development.

Maltreated adolescents who are homeless face a special separation problem: reexperiencing the stresses of earlier loss. Feelings of aloneness and anger, fears of abandonment, physiological reactions, acting out, and regressive behavior are common among young people who have not resolved the earlier separation from and loss of their biological parents. In an attempt to make sense of their current separation, such adolescents may regress into magical thinking—behavior common among children who have experienced loss. They may also become stuck in an earlier developmental stage or behavior pattern.[1]

Depression

Researchers have demonstrated that depression is one of the most typical psychological effects of maltreatment. Farber and Joseph studied the emotional and behavioral effect of maltreatment upon seventy-seven adolescents who had been physically abused.[2] They identified six distinct patterns of adolescent reactions, among which depression was the most common. Fisher and colleagues report that in a sample of physically abused adolescents 49 percent exhibited significant clinical indicators of depression.[3] Depression is the symptom most commonly reported among adults who were sexually abused as children, and this is empirically confirmed in several studies using clinical and nonclinical samples.[4] Although depression may be variously disguised, it is nevertheless the prevailing condition and must be addressed. Research has shown that maltreatment that begins during childhood and continues into adolescence may be related to greater depression during the teen years than maltreatment that started during adolescence.[5]

Low Self-esteem

The erosion of self-esteem is common among maltreated young people and is often associated with depression. At the time when the self-image was forming, such adolescents may have been receiving messages that caused them to see themselves as "worthless, crazy, bad people who have nothing valuable to say or contribute."[6] It is common for young people to engage in behaviors that reinforce a poor self-image—for example, they may act out or become difficult or withdrawn.

Maltreated young people typically blame themselves for the abuse they have experienced and develop a distorted view of negative events in their lives. Some tend to see themselves as responsible for everything bad that happens to them. This continuing distortion of reality contributes to low self-esteem, which can be immobilizing. Poor self-esteem both results from and contributes to a lack of success. For maltreated adolescents, survival alone has consumed most of their energy. They approach situations feeling inferior, even if some mask their uncertainty with an image of "looking good."[7]

Some adolescents may become compliant, often to the point of seeming withdrawn, lethargic, or as if they wished to become invisible. They are "understandably exhausted and to comply [is] an important survival skill—Don't object, don't complain, just sit [or lie] there and take it. They may also feel depressed and have a feeling of extreme deprivation. They may not have the interpersonal skills necessary to build or sustain satisfying relationships. They may be afraid to hope."[8]

Loss of Trust

Mistrust, particularly of adults, is common among abused adolescents. Experiences with their own parental figures have taught them not to count on adults for support, guidance, or protection. Many abused young people will "bite the hand that feeds them" to test an adult who is providing what their parents did not, or to recreate familiar, comfortable, though unhealthy family dynamics. According to Gil,

> When one cannot trust, a vicious cycle begins. The less you trust the less likely you are to have friends or intimate relationships. The more isolated you become, the less you can trust others. When others do not seek you out, or you cannot seem to make friends, you may think there is something wrong with you. Thus you feel more vulnerable, and more in need of guarding yourself rather than trusting enough to be open.[9]

Anxiety

Many maltreated teenagers are terrified of the mysterious underworld of their feelings. They do not have labels for their internal reactions and often experience all their feelings as a generalized state of anger and anxiety. They have an internal reservoir of anger that has developed from a long history of pain and rejection, and they are scared when the reservoir overflows under the stress of relatively minor frustrations. Whether they hold the anger in or explode, their feelings are unpredictable and frightening. Underneath the anger is pain, which makes these young people particularly vulnerable to additional disappointment and mistreatment.[10]

Denial

For some young people, their maltreatment history has been buried under layers of denial. Denial is a natural response to painful experiences. Much of the escapist behavior in which these young people engage, including drugs, alcohol, constant listening to music, sexual activity, and aggression, enables them to deny their maltreatment. Some may not actually deny the abuse, but rather will rationalize it ("My folks had a lot of money problems."), minimize it ("It wasn't really so bad."), and/or claim there were few or no negative effects ("I'm fine, it didn't really bother me that much."). But whatever the response, these adolescents devote a great deal of emotional energy to various forms of denial. They need to engage in a supportive therapeutic process that will allow them to risk giving up the protective denial and gradually recall the experiences and true feelings related to the maltreatment.[11]

Problems with Establishing Intimacy

Maltreated adolescents are frequently unable to establish peer relations and intimacy. Their capacity to understand and express their emotions may have been destroyed because their feelings were so often discounted. They may have been taught that they were not allowed to have or express their thoughts or feelings. The young person invariably assumes responsibility for the maltreatment in order to avoid seeing his or her parents as bad or unloving. It is essential for these young people to realize that the maltreatment was wrong and that it was not their responsibility or fault.

Feelings of Futurelessness

Many of these adolescents feel *futureless*. Their inexperience with competence and their expectation of being inadequate increase this feeling. They find it difficult to see beyond the present. They have little faith in the future because they have learned to expect little or nothing of what they hoped for as children. It is not easy for them to give up the comfortable view of themselves as worthless. This too is a loss and the young person has little confidence with a more positive self-image.[12]

Family Distortion

For adolescents who have been maltreated for some time, the concept of the family may have become distorted. Since family members have not met their physical and emotional needs, the family is not perceived as safe. Such adolescents have grown accustomed to an environment in which feelings of anger and fear are common. At the very least they are ambivalent about the family. Parents may have conveyed inconsistent and confusing messages—for example, love equals violence or pain, or love equals sex. There may be further distortion because the young person invariably assumes total responsibility for the maltreatment to avoid seeing his or her parents as bad or unloving.

As a result of these family distortions, many maltreated young people may have difficulty receiving help. Some will be grateful and open to assistance, while others will find it extremely difficult to accept that people can and will want to help.

Behavioral Effects

Maltreated teens often indicate their pain and hurt in ways that may not seem directly associated with a history of victimization. When a young person becomes involved in substance abuse or sexual acting out, treatment tends to focus on these specific problems, rather than on the underlying causes for the behavior. This is an important consideration to keep in mind as we examine the behaviors most typically associated with abused adolescents.

Common effects of maltreatment include poor impulse control and self-destructive dependency. Many abused young people, hoping that self-medication will deaden the emotional pain, become heavy substance abusers. They may engage in other typical acting-out behaviors associated with adolescence (for example, truancy and running away) and consequently experience trouble with authority. Some engage in more extreme behavior. Without proper intervention adolescents who have been abused may similarly abuse those younger or weaker than themselves. This is a particular risk in cases involving sexual victimization.

Some young people may engage in a mind/body split. Often victims of sexual abuse will not be able to recall details of the sexual acts but will be able to describe every detail about the ceiling and room. Some claim they believe their minds left their bodies so that they would not have to feel what was happening to them. Sanford suggests "given that the body, disconnected from the mind and spirit, absorbs the experience (as a self-protective device) it is not surprising that the body may later become the focus of symptomology."[13]

Sexual Acting Out

It is common for sexual abuse victims to become involved in sexual acting out. This can include revictimizing younger children, making poor choices of romantic partners, sexual precociousness, pregnancy, prostitution, or problems with sexual identity.

Recently, a great deal of attention has been focused on adolescent perpetrators—young people who victimize other children. An unknown percentage of sexually abused children become adolescent perpetrators. The victims are often the same age that the adolescent perpetrators were when their maltreatment began. Adolescent perpetrators are in urgent need of ongoing professional help. It is crucial that they receive the proper intervention services in order to protect potential victims. Such young people must be assessed as to whether they need inpatient or outpatient services. Several experts have identified conditions under which residential services should be considered.[14] Such services may be appropriate if the youth has

had previous treatment for a similar offense;

used violence, physical force, and/or threat of a weapon;

progressively increased the amount of force used;

engaged in bizarre or ritualistic acts;

displayed other antisocial behavior;

shown severe pathology to which the sex offense is secondary;

a chronic fixation on children rather than a regression attributable to an identifiable stress;

denied the activity or that the activity was inappropriate;

continued the offense despite the victim's expression of distress;

intellectual deficits that limit the understanding of his or her behavior.

Abused adolescents frequently make poor choices of romantic partners. Young people who have been abused or who have witnessed abuse often become involved in abusive romantic relationships. Such relationships can lead to another generation of domestic violence and abuse and can be extremely difficult to watch for those wishing to help. These relationships often defy logic as young women (and occasionally young men) seem unable to cut off relationships that are extremely violent in nature. One hopes that the recent popularity of "date rape" training will have some positive effect on the perpetuation of such behavior.

Perhaps the most dangerous behavior manifested by maltreated adolescents is prostitution. Both male and female maltreated runaways are at risk of becoming involved in prostitution. Boyer and James describe a four-stage process of involvement:

1. The *adaptation* phase. The young person is predisposed to prostitution through experiences (such as maltreatment and sexual victimization) that create a negative self-image, a feeling of being "spoiled" or "damaged."
2. The *acculturation* process. The young person begins to internalize the belief that a positive image can never be fulfilled. A pimp may further the commitment to prostitution by promising money, gifts, clothes, and love, and by threatening or beating the young person.
3. The *assimilation* phase. The adolescent accepts the identity of prostitute, adopting street language and culture.
4. The *commitment* phase. Finally, there is a permanent commitment to prostitution.[15]

Successful intervention becomes increasingly difficult as the adolescent progresses through these phases and becomes more involved in the lifestyle and culture. Typically, females involved in prostitution work for pimps, while boys tend to work alone or with peers. On the extreme end, these young people are at risk for violence, AIDS, and drug-related deaths.

Aggression

Maltreated adolescents frequently engage in aggressive and destructive behaviors. Some of them turn their anger inward, becoming depressed, or engaging in self-mutilation or self-destructive or suicidal behavior; others may turn their anger outward, becoming involved in repeated criminal activity that forces them into the criminal justice system where their abusive history may never be identified. Some young people who have been maltreated may need to have their aggressive impulses and behavior addressed by more than traditional counseling or therapy sessions; they may instead need a comprehensive program designed to address aggressive impulses. One such program is ART: Aggression Replacement Training, developed by Arnold Goldstein and Barry Glick.[16] The program can be implemented in both residential and nonresidential settings and it provides structured learning about appropriate and inappropriate behavior, anger control training, and moral education, all in a series of group sessions.

Control

Control can become an overwhelming issue. Those adolescents who have come from families in which control was a problem (either too much or too little) develop a variety of coping skills to get what they want from the world around them. Some may be extremely manipulative, while others may totally relinquish control by joining gangs, fanatic religious groups, or paramilitary organizations. Maltreatment and abandonment may result in "learned helplessness," a state in which a young person perceives him- or herself as unable to function in the most basic aspects of learning and socialization. Feeling they have lost control of their lives, they are often depressed. Alternatively, some adolescents attempt to control everything: "I don't need you—I can take charge of myself and can't count on adults." This attitude shows the importance of including young people in decision making and allowing them the opportunity to "be in charge." These young people need to be able to exercise control over appropriate areas in their lives and should receive training in effective problem-solving strategies.[17]

Victim Mentality

Many of these adolescents assume the mentality of a victim. They see themselves as the eternal victim and organize their lives around this premise. They may feel that they have been cheated out of their rightful due. It is important for these young people to feel empowered and to move from being victims to survivors. Gradually they must see themselves, with support, as responsibly taking charge of their lives. Although they may not get what they have missed in childhood, they can assume greater control over their lives.[18]

Suicide

Maltreated adolescents are at particular risk for suicidal thoughts and attempts.[19] It is essential that all who work with abused young people be trained in the handling of suicidal behavior. At the very least, staff should be familiar with the most common risk factors. Immediate action should be taken with young people who communicate suicidal thoughts and/or have a specific plan. According to Rotheram and Bradley, action should also be taken when three or more of the following risk factors exist:

The adolescent has previously attempted suicide

A close peer has committed suicide

A family member has committed suicide

The adolescent demonstrates antisocial behavior

The adolescent is male and depressed

The adolescent frequently abuses drugs or alcohol[20]

The young person should calmly be questioned about his or her self-destructive feelings—for example, "Have you been feeling suicidal?" "Do you feel like you want to hurt yourself?" Agencies should develop a plan or protocol to follow in the event of suicidal emergencies which includes a proven mental health expert for back-up and referral.

Survivor Guilt

Many maltreated young people act as if their families have established a ceiling on their futures. Some may believe that they are destined for a life of emotional disturbance, substance abuse, or violence. This worldview effectively prevents young people from being more successful than their families. Unconsciously, they view success as a criticism of their families' limitations—this is what Beyer describes as "survivor guilt." On the other hand, by perpetuating the family pattern, these young people are passively punitive; this, ironically, may be their only way to get back at their parents. So by fulfilling their destinies as failures, these adolescents achieve the dual goal of protecting their families and expressing their anger at them.[21]

Often abusing or neglecting families have no way of acknowledging the young person's success. In the mainstream culture, religious rituals and high school graduation offer opportunities for the family actively to encourage the adolescent to better him- or herself. The adolescent's guilt can be reduced if parents say, essentially, "We do not need you to be just like us." Helping professionals cannot effectively communicate this thought on behalf of the parents, although their encouragement of the young person's success has many other benefits. The young person needs both some encouragement for success from the family and help from others to overcome his or her survivor guilt.[22]

4
Interviewing and Disclosure

In this chapter we will discuss approaches to interviewing young people who have been abused. Interviewing in cases where there is suspicion of maltreatment is a highly delicate process. Creating a safe atmosphere that is comfortable and encourages openness is essential. Maltreated adolescents must believe that you are comfortable discussing the abuse. Many are extremely sensitive and can easily pick up any indication of discomfort. This becomes particularly important in cases of sexual abuse because of the nature of the language and the activities that are involved.

All individuals may not be equipped to deal with a disclosure or a young person who has been abused. Some people may have had experiences or feelings that could diminish their effectiveness with abused or neglected children. It is important to assess your own reaction and to know your feelings about the issue, given your own background and experience. Be certain you are prepared to respond appropriately. Spend time discussing the issue with someone with whom you feel comfortable. If you do not feel ready to deal with maltreatment issues, it might be helpful to work toward resolving your related personal issues.

When you do feel ready to deal with such issues, the following suggestions should help you obtain a clearer picture or more information regarding the suspected maltreatment. Throughout the interview process your manner of relating to the young person can ease this procedure and lay the groundwork for a more positive outcome.

Interviewing

When talking with a young person whom you suspect was abused, *use the utmost caution to avoid encouraging a false disclosure*. Although rare, false disclosures do occur, and therefore you must *avoid feeding words or ideas to a young person*. This means that your approach and its outcome are much more dependent on establishing a strong, trusting relationship that allows the adolescent to volunteer information about previous maltreatment.

The Interview Process

Develop Trust. Interview the adolescent in private and *spend time developing a relationship*. It is important to remember that any young person who has been maltreated has had his or her trust violated and may feel very vulnerable. The adolescent may have an impaired ability to judge trustworthiness and may test you in strange ways. Others, on the other hand, may be too trusting, which can lead to unrealistic expectations and disappointment. You may want to talk with the young person about the issue of trust, asking whom he or she does trust and why. It may be appropriate to discuss the concepts of earning trust, and partial trust.

Be Empathic and Nonjudgmental. Proceed in a slow and relaxed manner. Draw upon yourself and the uniqueness of the relationship you are establishing with the young person. Assess how you are being perceived and whether there is an adequate degree of trust. Ask yourself if you are just another person butting into his or her life, or someone with whom the young person would feel comfortable sharing personal information. If the former is true, then consult with supervisory staff for direction.

Assess the Young Person's Emotional Developmental Level. This is particularly important for maltreated adolescents because they so often come across as either very mature or immature. Consider their ability to describe or articulate their feelings as opposed to acting them out in destructive ways.

Learn How to Interview Boys. This may present a particular challenge because of the nature of perceived sex roles. All types of abuse, particularly sexual and emotional abuse, are seriously underreported among boys. Boys may find it more difficult to disclose abuse because of concerns about feeling and appearing sufficiently masculine. During adolescence, concerns about these issues are heightened and admissions of vulnerability may be seen as unmanly. In these cases it may be helpful to explain to the boy that talking about difficult situations and being maltreated does not mean he is any less masculine. You might want to educate him about how talking honestly about feelings shows another type of strength. Let him know that both boys and girls can be the victims of maltreatment by both men and women and that a young man's sexual preference is not determined by his victimization.

Proceed Slowly. Do not expect or feel pressured to obtain a great deal of information during a first or second interview. The fact that the adolescent is continuing to talk with you may be an important indication in itself and may allow you the luxury of time to develop a strong, trusting relationship.

Build the Relationship. In addition to formal counseling, casual contacts (such as driving, taking walks together, and so forth), may be useful for building a trusting relationship with the young person. As the relationship develops and more personal information is shared,

use active and empathic listening skills;

convey calm concern, interest, and respect;

attempt to offer what the young person will perceive as help;

assess the young person's emotional style and respond accordingly;

define the problem any way he or she wishes;

proceed at his or her own pace;

remain nonjudgmental.

Explain the Confidentiality Policy. Explain that everything discussed is confidential unless there is something shared that is related to the youth's safety and well-being, in which case the child protective agency will be contacted to help with the situation. Be certain to *explain and discuss your agency's confidentiality policy with the young person.* Assess whether dwelling on the issue will raise the adolescent's anxiety or make him or her feel more comfortable about discussing incidents of maltreatment.

The young person's perception of the situation is often crucial. Attempt to focus on the young person's perception of his or her family situation, role, history, and what is important in his or her life.

Don't be Judgmental. After you have established a relationship with the adolescent, you may wish to discuss those indicators you have observed. It is extremely important, however, that you present your observations *in a nonjudgmental manner, indicating your concern, not condemnation.* To use these indicators you might wish to attach those you have observed to feelings of pain, hurt, or fear the young person might be experiencing. For example, you might say something like this: "I've noticed that you've been sleeping a lot and not eating very much, and that's not like you. Sometimes when kids do that it's because they're feeling hurt about something going on in their lives. Why do you think this is happening to you?"

Be Aware of Nonverbal Reactions. During the interview *be aware of the youth's nonverbal reactions* (such as *flinching, changes in facial expression, stiffening, clenching of fists, turning away*), particularly at strategic points, such as when a particular family member is mentioned. Also, remain aware of your own nonverbal communication. Avoid giving the youth nonverbal messages that might convey a judgmental attitude or encourage a false disclosure of maltreatment information.

Consider Ethnic and Cultural Differences in Behavior, Language, Child Rearing, and Family Customs. It is your responsibility to educate yourself and remain sensitive to these issues. If you believe that you are not sufficiently familiar with a particular culture, request the assistance of someone who is. On the other hand, it is important not to stereotype or have unrealistic expectations when working with racially or culturally different families. Cultural issues and values should be taken into account when considering an intervention plan as well as an interview and assessment. Because of recent increases in immigrant populations from Latin American and Asian countries, your sensitivity to these issues is particularly important.[1]

Gather Information from Other Sources. You may wish to obtain information from other service providers with whom the young person has had contact. The proper release forms should be obtained. The adolescent's medical history can sometimes be of value. Look for previous hospital or doctor visits that may have been related to abuse, as well as for stress-related maladies such as migraines, ulcers, and so on. These stress-related maladies may be related to emotional maltreatment.

Use Art Forms. Some adolescents have great difficulty with verbal expression, particularly when it comes to feelings. For these young people, some art form can be a valuable communication tool, when used properly. If the young person feels comfortable drawing, this can be a most revealing medium. For those who feel self-conscious about drawing, cutting and pasting a collage from magazines is also a very good vehicle for communication. Other art forms for this type of expression include poetry, song writing, and dramatization. With all these art forms it is essential to discuss with the young person (to whatever degree possible) your understanding of what he or she was trying to communicate. Be aware that anything produced in this manner indicating maltreatment can be used as evidence in court. If you think that the young person's artistic expression is too difficult for you to work with, you might wish to consult with a creative arts or art therapist.

Use Humor Carefully. Some young people respond extremely well to humor. When you recognize this in a particular individual, you may use humor as a way of helping him or her feel more relaxed and comfortable talking. You should avoid directing sarcastic humor at the young person; rather, aim it at yourself or a nonthreatening situation. Be sensitive to his or her reaction to your use of humor or sarcasm, and take cultural considerations into account.

Making Additional Efforts. If you think that you have provided the young person with sufficient time and opportunity to discuss suspected abuse and still believe that maltreatment has occurred even though he or she has not discussed it, or if you think he or she may be in imminent danger, you may consider a more direct approach. Direct questioning, however, should be used only when you are fairly certain of your suspicions, and only after you have consulted with other staff, supervisors, and, when appropriate, child protective services. Again, you must be careful that you do not lead the young person or "contaminate the information" provided.

If a relationship has been established, and you continue to believe that the adolescent has been maltreated, it may be necessary to confront him or her directly. Do this gently and cautiously. Possible questions might include the following:

"Has anyone hurt you?"

"Did anyone touch you in ways that made you feel uncomfortable?"

"Did anyone force you or want you to do things that you felt uncomfortable about?"

"How are you punished when you do something your parents think is wrong?"

"How long and how often have you been responsible for the care of your younger brothers and sisters?"

"What are the rules in your house? How and by whom are they enforced?"

A confirmed response to these questions may not be sufficient for a report of maltreatment. You may need additional details to satisfy reporting requirements in your locality.

Assisting the Young Person with a Disclosure. When you think that the adolescent wants to disclose information about abuse but appears afraid, let him or her know that other kids have talked about these issues. Let him or her know that *talking about maltreatment to a counselor or responsible adult is the best thing that he or she could do* because

the abuse could stop;

protection and help will be available;

others, such as brothers and sisters, may be protected from future maltreatment;

others involved (including the abuser) might be able to obtain help.

Information-Gathering Techniques

The following procedures may help you obtain a more complete picture of the adolescent's personal and family history and of the constellation of family relationships within which he or she lives. Some may disclose direct or indirect information (in hints) about abuse during these procedures.

Timeline. One way to obtain personal background information, with the cooperation of the adolescent, is by developing a timeline. Draw a vertical line down a blank sheet of paper. Point to the bottom and indicate his or her birth. Ask what the young person knows about his or her birth and jot down any pertinent information or key words. Move slightly up the line to do the toddler years, preschool, and so forth. Alternately, you may wish to go year by year on up the line, marking each year and indicating any recollections the young person may have. The final three to five years may be the most detailed and may require additional paper or space. Here is a good question to ask: "Was there anything that happened to you when you were younger that you think is affecting you now?"

Genograms. Genograms are a type of family map capable of generating valuable family information while involving the young person. Begin by drawing a symbol for him or her at the bottom of the page. Females are circles, males are squares. Connect the young person to his or her parents with a T, connecting mother and father at the top horizontal ends with the young person at the bottom. Siblings are connected by additional vertical lines dropping down from the top of the T. The same should be done for each parent, stepparent, or significant household member. Go back as many generations as the adolescent can recall information about. A divorce is indicated by two short diagonal lines over the horizontal line indicating a marriage. A live-in relationship is indicated by a broken horizontal line. A death is indicated by an X over the representative circle or square. It can be very helpful to ask the young person to describe relationships, causes of divorces, deaths, and other important events in the family's existence. Often a family's recurrent themes, strengths, and generational patterns will become obvious to both you and the young person.

Learning about the Family Constellation. Try to complete the family picture by asking, for example, when and under what circumstances did older siblings leave home? What is the nature of the relationships with those children out of the home? Who constitutes the extended family? Who is around the house frequently? Identify major family events, such as births, deaths, accidents, marriages, illnesses, job losses or gains, moves, and so forth.

For the adopted and those in foster care: Check with the young person, current family, and social service agency for history of early maltreatment, including runaway incidents from foster placements.

Postdisclosure

After a disclosure (or after you think your suspicion needs to be acted upon), you must report the information to the appropriate protective agency in your state.

Your Immediate Response is Important. Frequently assess your own feelings and reactions to abuse and neglect in general. *Don't change your affect.* Avoid reactions of shock, dismay, or disgust. These convey your biases and judgments and may very well make the young person feel more anxious about discussing the maltreatment.

Find Out Why the Adolescent is Disclosing Now. Although reaching the point of disclosure may have taken a while, the adolescent has placed him- or herself in a position to share the information and receive help. Did the adolescent want freedom? Was he or she fearful for younger siblings? Was the abuse becoming more serious?

Validate the Young Person Unconditionally. Remain open to anything that may be said. This is usually not a problem; in some cases, however, it can be difficult since some adolescents have been so abused that they have become uncommunicative or unpleasant. They are hard to deal with but must be approached nonjudgmentally. They can be hostile and may become more so as you draw closer to painful issues.

Be Helpful. When dealing with a young person who is hostile or extremely withdrawn, *offer what he or she might find helpful.* Let the young person know that resolving the situation requires his or her cooperation. He or she may have a time frame that is different from yours, and think that disclosing or discussing the maltreatment is an important decision involving time and thought. For the adolescent who shrugs his or her shoulders and responds frequently with "I don't know," you might try asking, "What does 'I don't know' mean? Does it mean you really don't want to talk about it right now, or does it mean that you can't decide?"

Don't Presuppose Guilt or Anger. While you might expect a maltreated young person to have these feelings, neither may be present. *Avoid projecting your own reactions.* Be aware of your own reactions, and be sure to distinguish them from what you are perceiving in the young person. *Do not dwell on the alleged perpetrator.* Avoid focusing on the abuser or assuming that the adolescent has only negative feelings toward that person. (This is particularly relevant in cases of incest.) A young person may have strong family loyalties, even for the perpetrator, and these feelings should always be respected.

Getting Details. Without pressuring or prying, *get as many details as you see necessary.* The decision to obtain details should be carefully weighed. On the one hand, this information may help establish the young person's credibility when specific details remain consistent with each telling. However, do not have the adolescent repeat details because *he or she may often have to tell painful details to a variety of individuals.* In deciding how much detail and information to obtain, consider the ease with which the case will be accepted by the protective service agency or, if relevant, the court. Cases that are questionable for protective service acceptance may require more details than will clearer cases of maltreatment.

Give Reassurance and Support. After disclosure, the young person will need a great deal of reassurance and support. At this point it becomes important to *assess what feelings and issues he or she is dealing with.* These may include fears about the consequences of disclosing, physical and psychological damage, embarrassment, loss of trust and self-esteem, effects on the family, effects on peer and social relationships, guilt, ambivalence, and anger toward both the alleged perpetrator and the nonparticipating parent. Assess and explore with the young person any feelings of responsibility and assure the young person that what happened was in no way his or her fault or responsibility.

According to Linda Sanford, fear is one of the most common feelings following a disclosure.[2] She suggests that in helping the adolescent cope with these fears it may be most helpful for you to ask direct questions about the fears. Examples include: "Are you having any nightmares?" "Is there anything you worry about now in connection with what you've told me about what's been happening?" "What's the worst thing that can happen?"

Sanford goes on to say that "the fear may be a vague and overwhelming psychological phenomenon and clients cannot be expected to identify it on their own." Encourage expression of the fear through discussion or art, reassuring the young person that you can tolerate the fear, will not abandon him or her with it, and that it will not hurt or repulse you. As Sanford puts it, "Attend to fears on a concrete, problem solving, reality based level."

Anticipate Fears about the Outcome. Be prepared to deal with the young person's fears about the implications of the disclosure, such as "Who's going to talk to me? What do I have to tell them? If I talk to a cop, is somebody going to go to jail?" Let him or her know that you don't know exactly what will happen, but advise as to what you think may happen. Emphasize that "we will help you to be safe" and clarify your role in the overall intervention process.

Thank the Adolescent for Sharing Information. Let the young person know that you think that he or she did the right thing and that you will be available for future assistance.

The hours and days following a disclosure may be a fragile and sensitive time for the young person, who may be feeling a great deal of pain, guilt, and ambivalence, regardless of what he or she outwardly presents. Ongoing opportunities for crying, screaming, exercising, or general emotional and physical release should be created. The young person should receive special support, monitoring, and counseling during this period.

Young people exhibiting signs of serious depression, or those with suicidal backgrounds (previous or parental attempts), should be assessed and responded to for suicide lethality (degree of risk for completed suicide).

Here is a summary of interview guidelines. As you interview, try to avoid these pitfalls:

Focusing on the assault

Dwelling on perpetrator identity

Projecting your own feelings on the young person

Interrupting

Consider the following:

Degree of fear or shame

Guilt

Possible enjoyment, gratification, secondary gain (in sex abuse cases)

Real and perceived reactions of parent(s), relatives, and peers

Fears about what will happen to the young person and his or her family members

Degree of fear and depression

The Next Step: Intervention

Understanding the child protective and legal systems is essential for advocating effectively for young people in cases involving maltreatment. All suspected abuse must be reported to the appropriate agency. You should have as much of the required information as possible when you make a report.

The legal and social service systems' responses to abuse and neglect are based on state laws developed in reaction to federal child abuse legislation. Each state has its own set of laws that dictate how maltreatment should be handled in that state. It is essential that you become familiar with the laws and procedures in your locality.

The local child protective agency is required by law to investigate reports and determine whether a case is indicated (if it has some credible evidence of maltreatment) or unfounded (if the case has no credible evidence of maltreatment). When a case is indicated, the family may be offered services. When the family is uncooperative, services are refused by the family, or sexual or severe abuse has occurred, the courts may become involved.

When the young person is to be involved in a child protective investigation, intervention, or the legal system, it is important that he or she be adequately prepared for the process. Help the young person to understand what to expect, including what and who may be involved, and what the possible outcomes are. If the adolescent is capable, equip him or her with the tools to become a self advocate in the process by acquainting him or her with all available options and services.

The ideal child protective advocacy situation is a team approach whereby the program and other involved agencies clearly understand each other's roles, functions, and limitations. Each case should have a decision point process, where workers check in with one another and follow through on tasks. A variety of extremely effective coordinated team approaches exist in which a team of service providers meet to plan and coordinate services to abused young people and their families.

If a case is accepted by the appropriate child welfare agency, an appropriate service plan should be developed. Because maltreatment cases get so caught up in bureaucracy and legality, the ultimate goal of the intervention often gets lost. That goal is to provide the young person with what she or he will need to become a healthy, functioning adult. This must first involve a placement situation that assures the young person's safety. However, placement is only half of the picture. For any young person who has been maltreated, the psychological healing process is essential. Although there may be some resistance to this during adolescence, the young person should be encouraged to see therapy or counseling as a long-term, ongoing need. Some can benefit tremendously from such an experience during adolescence if the practitioner is acquainted with the emotional needs and issues related to a background of maltreatment.

Young people who have fled their homes and sought services voluntarily may need knowledgeable advocates to guide them through the various systems, to protect them, and to keep them off the street. The first step toward meeting the needs of these young people is to understand who they are, their pain, their strengths, and their experiences. The following life stories are presented with these goals in mind.

Part II
The Stories

Introduction

We have presented the preceding material to provide a framework for understanding issues of adolescent maltreatment and the stories that follow. We hope that the stories will bring to life the very real struggles of maltreated young people. Although they endured painful, traumatic, damaging events, they have against all odds survived, if not triumphed. These stories can be instructive about what happens to young people, how maltreatment affects their lives, but equally important, as a way to view the strengths and coping strategies that have facilitated their survival.

Jessica
(eighteen years old)

My mother was molested by her stepfather. She had his baby when she was fourteen, my brother Marvin, who is also my uncle. He's always been with my grandmother and is in the navy now. Then she got married to my father, but they were together a very short period of time. As a matter of fact, maybe not even two years. Because after my mother had my sister she got pregnant with me . . . me and my sister are like eleven months apart. They broke up while she was pregnant with me because my father use to beat my mother. My father was shooting drugs when I was born, he was an addict. I had to go through withdrawal, I was like four pounds, something like that. By the time my mother was seventeen, when she had me, she had three kids. I stayed with my grandmother for a while; how long, I don't remember. To tell you the truth I don't remember very much about my life before eight. Before that I can't remember very much.

The first time I ran away I was six years old. I'm serious. I was in public school and I was walking home. I thought a man was following me in a car. My aunt happened to be coming home and was in that car with him, but I didn't know that. I was like one block from my aunt's house. I was walking and she got out and started chasing me. I got home and got a beating anyway for running away. I just did it; I told myself that I was doing it because I wanted my mother to understand that I can see if I do something wrong. I was always the type of person where if I did something wrong, fine, I'll accept the punishment. But if I don't do anything wrong, I don't feel I should have to be punished and I will not be punished. I'll run away. I'll do whatever I have to. I don't feel that I should have to be punished.

Me and my sister use to take turns, you know, skipping school to watch my little brother while my mother worked. He was about four, maybe five—he wasn't in school yet. I had to be in maybe third grade. Nobody got on our case about that. At that time child abuse was a very serious thing but nobody was really noticing it, you know, nobody would say, "Oh, look at this child, she's being abused." It would have to be something with the child, the child itself had to put themselves in a situation as far as calling the cops, like I did. And my mother always held that against me. She always said that I was the one that brought the white man into her life. You see, when I was nine, I went into foster care for child abuse and neglect. I came home from school one day and I called my mother at her job. I told her that I had seen her money in the freezer and then asked her if I could go outside and play. I went outside and played for a little while and her boyfriend had came to the house. When he came to the house I didn't think much of it. I seen him go in, seen him go out, whatever. I went back inside, her money was gone. I called her at work to tell her, "You know, your money is not there. I don't know what happened to it." And she told me, "If my money is not there when I get back home you know you're going to get a beating." And you know I told her, "Why would I call you to tell you that the money was there if I wanted to turn right back around and steal it? If that was the case I never would have called you." She still stuck to her story, that if her money wasn't there when she got home, whatever. So I went to my grandmother's house, who lives right around the corner, and I stayed there for about an hour.

My mother called my grandmother to see if I was there, and my grandmother tells me, "You know I can't be in the middle of this—you have to go home." I went around the corner to the store and I started crying. This man asked me what was wrong and I told him. And he told me to call the cops because my mother used to beat us with extension cords. So I called the cops and I showed them the bruises on my arms and my legs and stuff and the next day child welfare came and they started doing an investigation. They put my sister and me in foster care. My brother Roland stayed home with my mother. We were in foster care for two years. We stayed with one foster family for maybe six months . . . and then another foster family for eighteen months. When we were in foster care my brother . . . I don't know what he did, he got bad. He began starting fights in our house, so he went to foster care about six months after we did. After two years of foster care we went to court and they sent us back home, but I didn't stay very long. I was about eleven and I stayed home for maybe two or three months. After that I ran away again, you know, because things weren't getting better. My mother was blaming everything on me. When we came back from foster care she had told the people in the court, "Well, everything is going to change, I want to be a good mother, I want to do this, I'm gonna to that, I'm not going to hit them." But you know that was what she was telling the man in the court and as soon as we got home it was something different. She would still hit us but not as much. She would wait until she got fed up and she would hit us, but it wouldn't be as bad because she thought that I would go back to the cops again. But she was still hitting us. You know everytime she had a streak of bad luck, "Oh, if it wasn't for Jessica I wouldn't be going through this." Whatever. She only did this with me because I was the one who called the cops. You know, so she figured it was my fault. So I was eleven and I ran away and they put me in SPCC, I believe, the Society for the Prevention of Cruelty to Children. I stayed there for a few months, about three months, and then I went to a diagnostics center and I stayed there for five months.

I didn't want to go home . . . and they always sent me back home. And I was always telling them, "What's the sense of sending me home when I want to run away again. I know things are not going to change." My mother, she'd be okay for the first few days, but then after that it's the same old thing. So I would just run away again. And they always wanted to send me back home. I was twelve years old and I stayed there for like five months. It was a bad place to go . . . the diagnostic center . . . it's where they send kids that they feel like they can't do anything with.

When I was there all the girls were like seventeen and eighteen and they had the gay girls there. Really tough-acting kids were there. It wasn't easy for me, you know, but God seen me through, he seen that I wasn't hurt, or nothing like that. I went through my little changes, you know, and I had to kiss a lot of behind in my days, but I got through. After the diagnostic center I went back home for about two weeks because the man told me, "You know your time is up. We can't keep you anymore." I called my mother and she told me to come on home. I packed my things and I came home and I stayed home for about two weeks. After that I ran away again. I don't remember why I ran away again . . . it seemed with me that my mother didn't have to say anything, it was her actions. I'm a sensitive person and being around my mother I felt if she couldn't show me that she loved me, then she didn't have to show me that she didn't love me. It was just things she did, her actions, how she would favor my sister more. I couldn't take that, I was really jealous. I just figured why go through all of this—I'd rather be in those places where the people don't care about me. I'd rather be with them because they don't care about me, they're not my family, then to be with my family and have them not care about me.

I could have went and stayed with my grandmother, but she's the kind of person who'll tell you right in your face you're not going to be no good. She said that maybe up to a month ago: "You're not going to be no good, you're not going to be no good." That's why I can't be around my family, you know, because if you're not giving me room to change or improve myself then I don't need to be around you because you're always downing me and you make me lose confidence in myself. When I'm doing good and my boss is telling me that I am working good—that makes me work harder. But when you tell me, "Oh, you're no good. I don't want to be around ya," I don't want to do nothing that will make you feel good because you're just gonna down me.

Where did I go? I went back to the agency I was dealing with when I was in foster care, and they sent me to a group home. I had just turned thirteen. I had met a guy, a Jamaican guy, who used to sell drugs. I used to go over there every night and come home at three o'clock in the morning. I was bad then, you know, and I got pregnant. At that time I was thirteen. My best friend—she was my roommate in the group home—got shot in the head. She got shot at my baby's father's place. I had went to my grandmother's for a visit, and I called the group home and they told me, "Don't come home; your roommate just got shot." She hadn't died yet 'cause she was in a coma in the hospital. She got shot the day after Christmas and she died January 7, on a Friday. They didn't want me to come home to the group home so I had to stay at my grandmother's for a while. Then when I finally came back I had to leave because I was pregnant, but I had a fight with a girl so that added flame to the fire. And they sent me to a place for pregnant girls. I stayed there for two days and both those nights I had nightmares, so the next day I left. I moved in with a girl named Gina—and I didn't know her from Adam and Eve. How did I find Gina . . . I don't know. God must have led me there because somehow or another I wound up in this girl named Roxanne's house. Roxanne got upset because she thought her boyfriend was looking at my behind. Well, there I was three months pregnant and she got upset because her boyfriend was looking at my behind! Now Gina was Roxanne's best friend—sounds like a soap opera, doesn't it?—and after she found out what happened she told me to come stay with her. The building she was living in had been taken over by the city so she wasn't paying rent. And I stayed with her up until I was about six months pregnant. I hadn't seen a doctor or anything. And I had started dealing with Gina's kid's father's brother. I was six months pregnant, I hadn't seen a doctor yet, and I had caught gonorrhea from this guy.

There was a lot of heat on my baby's father 'cause he was there when my best friend got shot. He didn't do it, but he was renting the place from this man. So when I got pregnant I decided to leave him alone. So we broke up. And I hadn't seen him since then. You know, when you're young you don't know no better and you get these no-good guys and he gave me gonorrhea and I didn't know it.

Then I went to the maternity program, you know, I just sat down and said to myself, "Pretty soon you're gonna be having this baby." I was thirteen and I didn't know what was going on . . . so I decided to call some runaway hotline. Somehow or another they referred me to the maternity program and that's when I found out that I had gonorrhea and the doctor told me, "Well, you know you got here just in time because it could have been spread to your baby." So I was lucky. And I stayed there from when I was six months pregnant until I had my son.

I never really thought of myself as being homeless . . . I felt like as long as I was under eighteen, Child Welfare was going to see to it that I had somewhere to go. That's the way I always thought, in terms like that. I knew somebody had to do something for me because I was under eighteen. I was well aware that that's pretty much how the system works, and I knew the things that I could do and get away with and what I could do and couldn't get away with. Like I said, I wasn't stupid, you know, I pretty much knew what I was doing.

After I had my baby, my mother called me and told me she was coming to see the baby, not me. When she came to see him he was supposed to be going in foster care that same day, which I didn't know. Nobody discussed it with me . . . no, they just told me that he was going. As a matter of fact, they had told my mother when my mother had asked them, "What is going to happen to the baby?" They told her—they didn't tell me. So she said, "Oh, no, he's coming home with me." All along she was telling me, "I'm not going to help you, I'm not going to do anything. You're going to be all by yourself." Well, she did take him home and then we went to court like the next week or something like that.

I was in the hospital for two days and then I went home for about a month. When I had came from the hospital—you know, my son was big, I had just turned fourteen when I had him and he was 8 pounds, 1 ounce, and 22 inches, and I had like twenty stitches. When I went home with my mother she had me working the same day. I was still bleeding and she wouldn't give me a rest and I couldn't take it. I had to get out so I went to my grandmother's house for about a month. And I came back and, you know, she started putting pressure on me. I can understand certain things she said, like she told me I couldn't smoke cigarettes. So for every cigarette I smoked I had to bring a can of milk, you know, different things like that. And to me that didn't make any sense. I can understand her telling me, "Well, look, you can't smoke if you can't take care of a baby," or something like that. But she was getting money for him and me and I was getting no part of it. She got everything. I had no income whatsoever. And yet still I had to go through all of this. When it came time for me to get shoes I had to ask my boyfriend and yet she wouldn't let me go out and see him. Okay, he could buy me shoes but I couldn't see him. What man is going to do something for you when he can't even see you? So I had to leave home.

I think she did these things to me just to see how much I would take, you know, to see how far she could go with me. Because when my mother took my baby for me it was a blessing. You know, out of all her kids, I'm the one she did the worst, but I'm the one that respects her the most. I will not disrespect my mother and I would let nobody else. All right, I love my mother dearly, but I just don't understand her. It was a lot of things you know—I know my mother had a hard life, she started having kids when she was thirteen—well, fourteen. I know it wasn't easy for her. But I figure that if you're a mother and you went through these things and you see a child getting ready to go through the same things, then you would try to help. You would sit down and say to yourself, "Well, wait a minute; don't you see something, don't you see that your child is going through something you went through?" and you're going to stop and you're going to say, "Wait—let's sit down and have a talk." My mother hasn't told me she loves me in I don't know how long. If my mother told me she loves me, I have to tell her first. Okay, that's the kind of thing it is with my mother. And I don't think that's right. She brought her kids up without showing any kind of love. For Christmas we got paper dolls with paper clothes. If my grandmother didn't get us nothing, we didn't get nothing for Christmas. Now my son is an altogether different story. She takes care of him very well, thank God, but with us, we had it hard.

My mother just had another baby, Lisa, who is one year old. In a lot of ways—well, as far as the kids are concerned, my son and her daughter—she takes care of them very well. She tries her best; I think she realizes that somewhere along the line she went wrong and maybe she's trying to make up for that. I don't know. 'Cause the way she's going now, pretty soon she'll be going to church because she listens to gospel music and what have you. I don't think she used to do that when we were younger. I came home one day and my mother was listening to a gospel station. That was a few years back, like about maybe three years ago, and I couldn't believe it. I didn't think my mother was the type.

Okay, so there I was, fourteen years old and I just had a baby. I'm living back at my mother's house for a while. One day, I went to the store and I'm going to lose her food stamps. I was too scared to call her now. My mother was smoking marijuana at the time and she gave me twenty dollars to go to the reefer spot to get some reefer. She also sent me to get some chitlins—those 10-pound things of chitlins—with twenty dollars in food stamps. Somehow or other I had went into the store to buy some loose cigarettes and I lost her food stamps. I had the twenty dollars cash, but I couldn't find the food stamps for the world. I called her and I told her, I said, "Look, Mom, I lost your food stamps. I got the cash but I can't find the food stamps." My little brother was with me, and I had the shopping cart and I hadn't bought the chitlins, and she said, "Well, send Roland home with my money and my shopping cart." She was in other words telling me I had better not come home. So I said to myself, "It ain't no sense in me giving him the cash when I'm going to need car fare for the train. I need food to eat." So I gave him the shopping cart and sent him home and I kept the money and I went back to Gina's house.

My son was almost two months, and it was a week before Thanksgiving. The day before Thanksgiving I met a guy from the Caribbean. I met him and went out with him Thanksgiving and I moved in with him two days later. Yes, and I stayed with him for about two months. He was very jealous and everything. He would give money to send my mother, but I couldn't go see her as often as I wanted to. And he asked my mother, could he marry me, because my mother had to give permission. And she told him yes, if he gave her two thousand dollars in quarters, nickels and dimes . . . that way they couldn't trace the money. Well, thank God something happened and we didn't get married. And I left him and I went back to Gina's house. I was fifteen then. I went back to Gina's house and I fell in love with some crackhead guy who was married named Ray and I had to get away from him. Then Gina turned right around and got on crack. Well I was on it too—I can't lie. I had always been smoking reefer. My mother always had it so I had to be about eight the first time. But you know I wasn't smoking it regularly, I didn't start smoking regularly until I got into the homes, which was when I was about eleven years old. But as far as the crack is concerned I had started that when I was like fifteen and then I had lost so much weight and everything. Ray was the person as a matter of fact that originally had me try crack. He started my best friend too. I never had to buy it. Gina, she has a daughter Larissa that's deaf, they owed her backmoney from Social Security, and when she first got this check we thought it was $11 but it was $1,100. And that is where all the money went.

I was on welfare at the time too. After I had got off my mother's budget, we went down to Gina's social worker and we had gotten me on Gina's budget. Gina would always tell these lies. One time she told her boyfriend that her daughter had thrown her money out the window; another time somebody picked her pocket. But you know, the money went to drugs. She had all this paraphernalia in the house and her boyfriend always thought it was me, he never suspected her. So me and him would get into big arguments and she could never say nothing because she knew she had just as much fault in it as I did. You see, I wasn't the type where I'd say, "Oh, boy, I got to have it." It was just a thing with me; because it was there I just did it.

I finally left her and I moved in with this guy Charles. I knew Charles for about two months before I moved in with him. Charles was the worst man that I have ever had in my life because I had to go through so many things with him. He used to sell drugs—he didn't sell it but he had people sell it for him. For the first few months after I moved in everything was fine. I had the world, he gave me everything I wanted. But I couldn't go out . . . I could do whatever I wanted to, but I couldn't go out of the house.

He was very jealous. For some reason or another I always wind up with these jealous men. We were living in this little hallway room, a very little hallway room—it was really small. We stayed there for about two months and we used to have arguments and fights. He used to beat me up pretty bad. I didn't do anything. I would lie on the bed and say, well, tomorrow morning as soon as he leaves I'm leaving, or I'd say, tomorrow morning as soon as he leaves I'm going to call the cops. By tomorrow morning I was not mad anymore. I think I was just too scared to leave him, you know. At that time I was too scared to leave him because as far as I was concerned he was the best man I had ever had because he gave me everything I wanted. But he wouldn't let me do anything.

At first he didn't beat me. It wasn't until one night I left him and went to my friend's home who had lived in the same building as Gina did. Charles came looking for me that next day and when I went home that same night he busted my lip. Yeah, my tooth was sticking to my lip. I went back to Angie's house but three days later I went back to Charles and we moved to a new building. It was there that we got on drugs. At first he was selling the crack, and then we started smoking the crack and everything. I say we blew $50,000 you know . . . we seen money come and go constantly. I used to try to tell him to put the money away, you know. There were times where we would stop for days, and somehow or another he let somebody talk him into it and we'd go right back into it. If he started, he had to make me start. If I didn't start then I was turning against him, you know, I didn't want him no more, and then he'd get real crazy. So it had got to a point where I was scared to tell him no. I didn't know how to answer his questions depending on what mood he was gonna be in. It got so bad that I had tried to hurt myself. I was trying to hit myself in the head with a Pepsi bottle so I could bleed so that somebody would come and get me. I had lost so much weight I must have been about ninety some odd pounds. My whole food list consisted of potatoes, eggs, margarine, and Carnation milk, and bread. That's what I lived on.

He had gotten on drugs and busted my head, stabbed me in the hand with a pen, beat me with extension cords—everything. Believe me, he beat me so bad that one day I couldn't move. He went and got a bucket and bathed me and cleaned me and told me he loved me, and I'm sitting up there saying, "Oh, God, how could you, Jessica." It wasn't serious, I made it worse for myself. Because I could have left but I think I was so dependent on him that I felt that if I left him nobody would want me. I wouldn't be any good, you know, I wouldn't be worth anything. So I decided I'm gonna stay with him, I'm gonna stay with him. But when I finally did leave him, if I hadn't left him at the time that I did, I probably would have been dead. He was on drugs so bad. I don't think I was hooked because he was on the drugs so bad just seeing him doin' it I wouldn't—I couldn't. But then if I didn't do drugs, he would think that I was turning against him and he would want to beat me again. So I had to. I would say he was keeping me on drugs to have me there depending on him just so I wouldn't leave.

A lot of pretty strange things happened. During the time that Charles was selling drugs we had gotten into a case with the special state prosecutor. What happened was we were selling cocaine and an off-duty detective tried to rob us. He was going to shoot my boyfriend. They was on the floor and they rolled on the ground outside, you know, rumbling around. The detective was trying to pull the trigger and my boyfriend was pushing it. And I had just bought a Pepsi (that was my drink) so I emptied it and I hit this policeman over the head. We didn't think he was a real policeman because at first when he told me to go downstairs I expected to see all these cops, you know, handcuffs and everything. I went downstairs and I didn't see this so I just figured, you know, hey, he's not a cop. Charles wound up beating him up. The only thing I did was hit him in the head with a bottle. It was my boyfriend and C.C. who had beat him up. But when I seen him get ready to shoot my boyfriend, I hit him in the head with the bottle. After that we ran and left him there. There were people who had witnessed it and knew where we lived, right, and they told the cops. The cops must have been waiting for us to come downstairs. I happened to go downstairs to see what was going on. The cops just grabbed me, handcuffed me, and searched me, and they took me down to the precinct. At first they didn't know that there was a cop who had come and took drugs from us. They thought that we was trying to rob him. I hadn't slept for like two days. They have our confessions on videotape, so when they were videotaping me, I kept drifting in and out of sleep. I was sitting up but I kept drifting and they would call my name and I'd go, "Huh?" When I went to testify they asked me how long had I slept when they did the videotape. So when they had me in the precinct, they fingerprinted me. I was sixteen. I was talking to this cop and I told him everything that had happened, how the cop had come upstairs and I opened the door and he told me to go downstairs. Then the precinct cop told me, "Well, you know, you should ask to speak to the narcotics sergeant." When I did speak to the narcotics sergeant I told him the story. I came to find out that this same man, the same cop we had beat up, they had been suspicious about him going to drug spots and taking things from people. So the case turned around, it was used against him. I happened to get lucky.

We then started going down to the Special State Prosecutor's Office, visiting this man Dave. Every week we would go down there and they would give us twenty dollars or thirty dollars, you know, telling us we would have to testify about what happened. They knew we were on drugs. They could tell because every time they came to see me I always had on the same green suede skirt. It was very expensive, and was the only thing I had kept out of all my things that had not gotten ripped. I used to always wear slippers down there, never shoes, you know. Thinking about it now I realize how bad I must have looked because I didn't know these things. When you're on drugs, you're just dazed, you don't know nothing. God, now when I think about it, I feel so embarrassed. Anyway, these cops turned out to be good friends, you know, Mr. Parriso, and Mr. Smith. They knew that Charles was beating me up too, but if I wouldn't press charges there was nothing they could do for me. They couldn't help me.

Well, my family used to come and see the surroundings and everything and they would know things weren't right. But as long as I would tell them, "Hey, look, everything is okay, you don't have to worry about me, I'll be alright" . . . they wouldn't bother.

I did manage to leave Charles a number of times. One time I left Charles in January and when I left the house I had on a black skirt with no stockings with shoes, I had on a coat with a hole on the side from the heater, and I didn't have on no shirt, I just had on a bra. I had to get out of the house and I took the train and went to a runaway shelter. That was one of the times I had left him. Another time I left him when my sister came and got me, when I was on the drugs. She hadn't been around for a while, and I kept saying to myself, I kept praying, "Please let her come by," and I just had a feeling that that week she was gonna come. I was telling Charles, you know, "The very next person that comes here I'm gonna make sure they get me out of here because you will not kill me." And she came and I told her, you know, "I want you to go downstairs and call the cops. I want you to tell them to come and get me." I stayed up there with him and he heard me telling everything. When she went downstairs he knew she was going to call the cops. He was telling me, "Please don't go, everything's going to change, you don't have to worry, you know, everything is going to be the way it used to be." But I couldn't believe him no more, so I just said, "Hey, look, just let me go." So I went to my mother's and stayed there for a while. But I went back to him. We moved into a very nice apartment on Manchester Street, a very nice apartment. We had brand new furniture, TV, VCR, everything. And we were there for a couple of months. But he got back on the drugs again and this was the last straw. You know, here I am sixteen years old with this nice apartment, full refrigerator, I didn't want him to get back on the drugs again, that was the last thing I needed.

He had been selling and not using. Then he had started using again. I always knew when he was using drugs because, you know, he would come in and he would just be so paranoid. He went to the mirror and he said, "Wow, don't you see these snakes crawling on me?" I said, "Oh, God, here it goes again." He was really going crazy 'cause he was on his drugs and he was saying that shadows were in the house and he had mirrors all through the house. He took the doorknobs off the door, took away the knives, the forks, the spoons so I couldn't pry the door open. He put bars on the window with bottles on top of the window . . . he was so paranoid. He would sit the Pepsi bottles on the window like a pyramid, okay, so if someone was trying to come in through the window the bottles would fall down. But sometimes the wind blew the bottles, okay, and they fell down. Oh, God, that was it, and I mean there were times I would just have to sit and pray to God, you know—don't let those bottles fall, please don't let them fall. And, oh, God, it was bad, you know. What did I do? I called his brother, Michael, and Michael came down and I said, "Look, I am leaving him." And I left him that night. I went to some big runaway shelter. But then, Michael came and got me and told me come back to him. "He's not going to do it again," he promises. Well, he did it the same night. He went back on drugs the same night. And when he went to sleep, I got up and I packed only what I had bought. I didn't take nothing he bought me, you know, I made sure he had no reason to come looking for me. I didn't steal; the only thing I took from him was car fare to get back to the runaway shelter.

So I went to the runaway shelter and he kept coming there looking for me. They wouldn't tell him anything but he knew I was there. He must have stood out there for hours in the cold, just waiting for me to come out there. I would come out sometimes to smoke a cigarette or something and he would still be standing there. So I couldn't go nowhere. They moved me over to another shelter. I had turned sixteen and they had moved me over to a temporary group home. Somehow or another he found out where I was—he must have asked one of the kids over there and they must have told him. He came to the shelter at three o'clock in the morning telling them that I was in a crack house. We was at the group home talking to this lady from the main shelter that night. And he rang the bell and he called out for me. I knew it was him, I just knew that voice, and I ran downstairs. He told her he was a counselor from the main shelter and I told her, "Don't open the door, don't open the door," and she said, "Why?" I said, "He's not who he says," and then he told her, "I am here in reference to Jessica Brooks, she's in a crack house and I just want to talk to you and let you know," and she said, "I can't let you in," and then he said, "You just tell her that when she comes out here tomorrow morning she's dead." And he had a paper bag; they said it look like he had a gun and I'm not sure if he did or not. Knowing Charles, he did. And I stayed up all that night. I wouldn't go to sleep. All the girls in the house were crying because he really threatened me. The cops came and everything and after that they told me, "If we keep you here, we are jeopardizing a lot of other girls because we don't know how crazy he is." So they had to send me away from there. And somehow or another they got me to go into Job Corps earlier than I was supposed to.

I had been waiting to get into Job Corps . . . one of the counselors set it up. I was sixteen when I went to Job Corps. I was there for five months and three weeks. I had started gaining my weight back and everything, I started rebuilding again. I liked it as far as education was concerned. I always kept up on my reading—my reading and my math, everything is up to date, so I always kept that up because I always love school. I don't mind going to school, and I know getting my GED would not be a problem for me. When Job Corps found out that I hadn't been to school in like three years they couldn't believe it. They couldn't understand it and didn't believe it until they got my records from junior high school that I hadn't been to school all that time. I would go to the library and sit down sometimes for hours. Even now when I am working I try beating the computer, you know, I always try adding in my mind, like I turn my head and think about it.

But the environment of Job Corps I couldn't deal with. It was too clean. There were some things I liked, like getting up in the morning, seeing the deer at your window and the raccoons and groundhogs and stuff like that. But you know . . . I didn't finish the program. I had 63 percent of my trade and one week left to take my GED. I didn't leave, I got terminated. There's one thing about me, that's always been known throughout my records, that I have sort of temper tantrums. I am very easy to get along with but then there are times when I don't take to certain people. Like I just might look at a person and say, "Oh, no, that person is not right," or something about them, you know, I don't like. I can tell the sort of person that in front of a counselor she'll be all good and everything but behind the counselor's back is another person.

For some reason I got terminated. The thing was—I had dreads and in the cafeteria they state that you're supposed to cover your hair, you're not supposed to have any scarfs or anything and I'm not supposed to have my hair out. I am not supposed to show my hair to nobody but my husband or my boyfriend. And when I came to the cafeteria they would have this big fit about "Oh, you have to take off your hat" and I got a lot of write-ups about that. They were giving write-ups. And then I had got a pass from the assistant director stating that I was allowed to wear my hat in the cafeteria and then it turned into a lot of different things. I think what really bothered the staff was that I knew how to get to them without disrespecting them. And that's what bothered them because they would get a lot of kids upset and then they would just go crazy. Me, on the other hand, I don't know, I find my little ways but then the other times I get out of hand too.

Anyway, I got terminated along with another friend and we went back to the runaway shelter. The shelter told us that they couldn't help us because it was Job Corps' obligation to see to it if they terminated us that we had somewhere to go. We called Job Corps back to tell them that and Job Corps told us that their only obligation was to see to it that we had a bus ticket to get to the city. But the runaway program couldn't accept that. They sent us to another shelter, and at that place me and my best friend got into a fight . . . So they sent us back to the main runaway shelter who gave us overnight shelter and said they couldn't help us no more. Then we went to another shelter. I was seventeen. I stayed there for about three weeks, maybe a month, and then they told me my time was up. I had gotten into a little thing with this lady Jackie over there because I was laughing at their drug addicts. Their drug addicts were starting trouble with us and I have this really annoying laugh and they got upset over that. So they called my social worker who I didn't know from Adam and Eve and he sent me to a diagnostic center run by the church. My counselor at the diagnostic center then referred me to Project Teen Hope, which is really another runaway shelter. And I came there and I was there for about a month. What happened was I got high. I got caught and was put on restriction that weekend, but I didn't stay on restriction. And that Monday the staff had this nice long talk with me and I promised them that they didn't have to worry about me getting high anymore. That same day me and a friend got high off some acid and that next day I left, they made me leave the program. I think everybody was upset with me when I had got kicked out. I knew I had done wrong, you know, I knew it. But I didn't think that it was gonna be a great big setback or drawback or anything that was gonna mess me up. Why . . . I don't know, I just don't know why I did it. I wouldn't say I was feeling down or that I was depressed or anything like that. I just felt like, "Hey, you're turning eighteen soon, honey, and if you don't have no place to go, then that's it for you. You'll have to find some place on your own." I wasn't saving no money all this time that I was working. I wasn't doing anything, I was just spending my money like somebody was giving it to me and saying, "Here, do as you please." And that was another way that I messed up.

But at the time, I was in one of those stages where I felt like, you know, I knew I was going to be eighteen soon, but like I said I wasn't eighteen yet. And as long as I wasn't eighteen they had to have somewhere for me. When I went to that bad place, they'll tell you I was so depressed, the two weeks before I turned eighteen, I was so depressed because I felt that once I turned eighteen that that was it for me. That I had no life, that I had no future, that that was it. Once I turned eighteen everything came crashing down because nobody was going to help me.

Then I went to this other group home. Take it from me, don't send nobody there because they don't care about anybody. All black staff and they don't care about anybody. They are worse than any other place I've been. You know, when your time is up they tell you, "Well, don't worry, we're doing everything we can." They are such phonies, you know what I mean. And I had turned eighteen.

From there I tried to get into another group home, this independent living program, but there was no guarantee that they were actually going to take me. I had to plead with Mr. Johnson to take me. He told me I could move in and I've been there ever since. I've been working, you know, and I am trying to get in school. This is a very good independent living program. They had an apartment building renovated. The apartment we're in is the only apartment in the building with two floors, a spiral staircase, you know, modern kitchen, one and a half bathrooms. It is adorable. I have my own room, privacy, you know. The girls—we have our problems. Our biggest problem right now is sharing chores. Right now I am the only one in the house working. Everybody gone and quit their jobs. I have been at my job four months.

Some people helped me along the way, like some of the people at Project Teen Hope. But I got to the point where when I am in a program I always feel that I'm just a number. I don't believe that they are gonna treat me as one specific case because they've found out that I have been in all these different placements, I don't feel like they're gonna treat me any better. I happened to get lucky when I left Project Teen Hope, because when I left there I made a very big mistake getting high and I knew it. Doing what I did, I had enough sense to know better. That's why I know when I left everyone was very disappointed with me. Because they knew that I had enough sense not to do what I did, and I knew it also.

I feel that a lot of the places I've been to, the people don't really care as much as they try to put on that they do. Like I know that when it is time for inspection, the night before is when they start buffing the floors, and cleaning out the bathrooms and all of that, you know. That shows me that they don't really care. Because why wait until the day before inspection, why not do it every week or every month? The day of the inspection the kids are treated so well, they are given special privileges for the day. I noticed that and I don't like that. That's why if I was to have anything to do with social work, if I went into any kind of field, I would go into the field of busting these phony places. I would because they have a lot of phonies, so many phonies. And I just can't see that. You'd be surprised that the kids who's gotten beaten worse than me come into these places thinking they're really gonna get help and thirty days later they're put out the door. That hurts. And they say to themselves I might as well go home and get beat, at least I have somewhere to go. And I would hate to see that happen. Bust these phony social workers, these phony places who claim they really care. Speaking honestly, Project Teen Hope is one of the best runaway shelters. You can tell when somebody cares when you can see the tears in their eyes when they say, "Jessica, you have to go." But you know when you do something wrong you do something wrong. But you can tell when people care. You can tell when somebody is putting on an act or when they're not, when they're lying and things like that. But that other group home, they're phonies. Most other group homes, they're phonies, they care about nothing. You know what it is with the big places . . . they have seen so many kids that don't want to improve themselves, the kids that do want to improve themselves, they don't believe them. They treat everybody the same, you know, they're all the same. That's how they are, they're all the same kids and they're never gonna change. You'd be seeing kids who just ran away from home and in shelters for the first time, you know, and they treat them really bad. They'd be crying at night, I mean sleeping on the floors, on mats and everything, getting up at six o'clock in the morning eating cold cereal and then having to look for a job. If they don't have a job by two or three weeks then they have to leave.

My friend, you know, she knew some guy in one of the group homes. It didn't start happening until I had left, though, and she had stayed. They had started smoking reefer together and having sex on the couch and in the kitchen. She told me 'cause I talked to her on the phone. She was, like, "Jessica, guess what, me and so-and-so did this." And I said, "What?" She doesn't lie to me. We tell each other our deepest, darkest secrets. I know she wouldn't lie to me about such a thing 'cause she is not that kind of person. I don't know, I couldn't see myself doing that, you know, because I mean, he couldn't even help her. I mean, what could he do for you. Here you are laying out with this man who's gonna go home to his wife and kids like nothing happened. Yeah, he was a staff member. Couldn't even give her a good recommendation to another place. I said I would do that for a good recommendation but come on, he did nothing. She was just laying out with this man who was old enough to be your father. Even though they reported it . . . the guy is still there.

At that place we got treated like we were twenty. We were allowed to go out every day and we made excuses, like, "Oh, we've got to do this for our job," and they knew darn well that at seven o'clock at night what could you possibly do for your job. And you know, they would let us go out and everything and we would come back at least by ten o'clock. He said one day, "Yeah, I like young girls." I don't like no old man messing with me, I think that's disgusting.

Then my best friend left me because she fell in love with some guy. She found some old half-assed boyfriend and totally forgot about me. So that showed me you can't trust nobody. If you can't trust your best friend, you can't trust nobody. That really messes up your mind when you say, you know, you think you really have a friend and then they do something to you, that only made me feel like, there it goes again, everytime you trust somebody, they do the same old thing. Right now, I don't trust anybody, okay. And I'll tell the person, "I don't know you and I don't trust you. And the same way I don't trust you, I don't expect you to trust me. I don't want you to trust me. I don't expect you to trust me because I don't trust you." It's been like that for so long, I just don't trust nobody, I don't look for people to trust me. Out of all the places I've been to, I've never been known as a liar, and I've never been known as a thief. And that is another thing I thank God for because I can always, if I need a reference from a group home or from a diagnostics center, from a runaway shelter, I can always call them. I know they will always say, "Well, she did have a little attitude problem, but that was about it."

There's been days when sometimes I think that maybe there's something more to me, because I analyze myself. I get up in the morning and I start thinking about certain things . . . the other day that I got up, I was talking to myself and I said to myself out loud, "That's a good sign of going crazy—you might as well go to a psychiatrist." Then I'll be saying to myself, "Well, what's the sense of you going to a psychiatrist when it seems you already know what he's going to tell you." That seems like a problem with me because I always try to predict what's going to happen before it happens. For me it can lead to a problem because if I feel something good is going to happen, then it doesn't happen, then I'm really disappointed in myself because then I say, "Oh, you're not as smart as you thought you were." Or then if I think something bad is going to happen and something good happens, then I say, "Well, you were lucky."

There used to be a time where I didn't believe in God. I'm not going to say I didn't believe in him; I didn't want to admit that I believed in him. I would tell people, "Oh, I'm an atheist, I don't believe in God. How can you believe in somebody you don't see, he doesn't do anything for me." Now, I believe in God. I accept him more now . . . I went and bought my Bible and I read a chapter a night and pray. I don't always read a chapter a night, sometimes I go for days, I may go to sleep without, but I always say that little prayer. There was one morning I really thought I was going to pay because I got up and I had forgotten my Chapstick, then I remembered, and I said, "Thank God." And then I had forgot my work clothes but I remembered and I said, "Thank God." I forgot to take out the garbage and I kept saying all that morning, I kept saying, "Thank God, thank God." And I had such a wonderful day that it just made me, you know, it made me see that he has a big part to play in my life. And I don't know, a lot of people may say, even my mother-in-law tells me, she says somebody who's been on the streets for so long, it's a good thing that you're not dead, in jail, or on drugs. You know, but I do believe I was one of the lucky ones. I really do believe that for each mistake I made it taught me not to make the same mistake again. I always make mistakes but never the same one. I have yet to make the same mistake, not yet.

I feel like a lot of my life I've been a victim, because I always tried to be a good person. The harder I tried the worse it was, the worse things happened. And I didn't even know which way to turn, what to do to make things better. I was always too young to do what I wanted to do, but yet, too smart in the head to do it. Like in a lot of places I was a victim there too, because they always treated me different because I always seemed more mature. But then when I always wanted to do something that I felt I could do, I couldn't do it because they would say I was too young. And that confused me. Because if you're telling me, "Oh, you're a very mature person," and then when I want to do something mature, you know, I'm too young. It doesn't make sense, you know, what are you telling me? I never did understand things like that.

When I was in Job Corps, I asked them to let me see a psychiatrist. He helped me in a lot of ways. Because I had already said to myself, "When you go see this man, you know, you have to tell him everything." They don't help—I think they help you to help yourself. That's what he did. He made me realize a lot of things and I think that helped me. I wouldn't see a psychiatrist now, but if I ever get rich enough to afford one I just might. I know that the things that happened in the past, I don't let them get me down. And I give everybody a chance. Like I said, I don't trust nobody but I give everybody a chance. I won't say, "Oh, well, you're just like the rest," I won't say that until you prove to me you're like the rest.

I was always treated like I was older than everybody else even if I wasn't. I always acted older than everybody so I was always treated different. But then, you know, after a few weeks, they started treating me like everybody else. I didn't want to be treated differently than anybody because like I said, you confuse me when one moment you treat me like a child and the next moment you treat me like an adult. I don't understand that. It can confuse anybody when you have them on this up-and-down scale of how you want them to be and they try to live up to your expectations but they don't know what to be. I don't know when I come around you whether to be a child or to be an adult. But that's a lot of ways the group homes and programs are messed up. I'm the type of person that if you are phony I'm gonna tell you you're phony. I'm a very outspoken person. If I have something on my mind I am gonna tell you. And that has gotten me in a lot of trouble at times with a lot of different places because I am gonna tell you. You can sit there and tell me you care all you want but deep down inside, you know, they don't care. When I've seen on my folder this number, I really hate that. I hate that so bad that they can't just use our names, instead of having to use that number. I really hate that.

Sometimes I feel responsible for all the things that have happened to me. But now I don't. I know I had a big part to play in it because I wasn't no angel. I'm not an angel now. I used to feel responsible. I used to say, "What are you doing, what is it that you are doing?" I would actually sit down and write out the things I did to see what I was doing wrong and I just couldn't see it. You was just born at the wrong time. But then I felt, my mother was a victim too because of all the things she went through. I know that she had a hard life herself, you know, and in a sense I can sympathize with her. But then in a sense I can't because I figure if you had a hard life, you wouldn't want to see your children go through the same thing. My mother still has a pretty cold heart. My youngest brother, Roland, right now he is in a prison in another city; he's been there since he's been about ten. He will not come home for a visit and I feel the only reason that he won't come is because she won't call him and she won't say, "Roland, I miss you, I love you, I want to see you, could you come spend the weekend with me." Every time he came home she wants him to clean, clean, clean. He's a young boy, he doesn't want to clean, he wants to play. I can understand having chores, but to make him keep running to the store, like my mother used to make me cook breakfast for her husband. The last time I went to visit her, I told her, "If I come over there and if I help you do any cleaning, I'm not cleaning you and your husband's room, I'm not cleaning any windows, and I'm not shampooing any rugs." Because my mother won't do it. As long as she knows you'll clean, she won't. And then after she gets high, whatever you clean, she goes back and messes it right back up. And people get tired of that. He's a young boy, he doesn't want to clean all the time. Let him have some kind of fun. You know why she won't call him? She doesn't want to run up her phone bill. That's not good, that's just not good.

I would say that I've gotten stronger from all the things that have happened to me by not giving up. I got stronger because I just never gave up. That's why I said somebody's guiding me. There were times when I preferred to be dead. I tried to commit suicide about three times. One time by the pill . . . I was about fourteen after I had my son. I took about forty Anacin 3's and I called suicide prevention and, you know, I don't think I really wanted to kill myself. I just think I wanted somebody to notice me, to say, "Well, you know, she's tried everything; what else can she do?" I went and bought the pills and I called suicide prevention and I was talking to some lady and told her what I did. We kept talking and then the money finally ran out and I couldn't talk no more. Before I could get out the door, I hadn't fainted yet, the ambulance was there. Another time I tried to stab myself in the arms with a steak knife, and another time I think I tried to drink myself to death.

There were times when I had given up; I just let time, you know, let time take its course. Things change, how I don't know. I would just tell anybody, things are going to go bad, but don't give up, it's not just prayer that's gonna help you, it's believing . . . believing in God, really believing because, you know, you can pray tonight and if you don't mean what you saying, you're not getting any help. But if you mean it you're gonna be helped. Times are gonna seem hard, believe you me, I've been there, and I know what it is like, I been through everything from drugs to every kind of home, from men beating me and everything. But I didn't give up, why I don't know, but I think that my time hasn't come yet. But when it comes I'm gonna be okay. All these years of hurt and trouble and rocky roads, it can't be like this forever, I know this can't be forever.

Another thing that has kept me going is my son. I don't wish I had an abortion or anything like that. In a lot of ways I wish I hadn't got pregnant, because it messed me up. It gives my mother reasons to use everything against me. Now it doesn't hurt me in any kind of way. But there was a time when having a child really hurt me, you know, 'cause fourteen years old with a child, nobody wanted their kids around me, not that I really cared because I wasn't playing with no fourteen-year-olds at that time anyway. But there's a lot of things to it.

In my own life I don't think there was nothing I could have done differently, no matter how I tried. I tried, and I know I tried, there was nothing I could do differently. 'Cause each place I was at there wasn't no place else I could turn, so I had to kiss ass, do what I had to do. That was just the way it was for me. I didn't have no other choice. If I met a kid in the same situation like I was in, I would want to tell them, if your parents are abusing and neglecting you, get away from them, and don't think that because you leave them that that is the end of your kissing ass 'cause it's not. I'd also tell them not to be like me and get into a good place and then mess up.

I do not regret making that phone call when I was eleven. Because if I hadn't have made that phone call, then instead of me just having one child I probably would have three by now and on my way to having another one. When I had my son, I decided no more for me. It wasn't the pain that made me not want to have another, but what is the sense in bringing one child in the world and then bringing another and another. You see the first one can be understood as being—you got pregnant by a mistake, not saying the baby was a mistake, but you got pregnant not knowing what you were doing. The second time is no mistake; no matter what you tell me, it's no mistake. I don't know, to give anybody else advice it's gonna be a lot of things that they're gonna go through but everybody has their price they have to pay for life. And just do the best you can, you know. Just try as hard as you can; you can always say, I tried, and that'll get you far. Trying gets you far. It is better to try and fail than not have tried at all. I always learned that.

The one thing I want to do is finish school, because I know I am smart. My records prove that as far as school is concerned I am very smart. I don't have to worry about that. I am street smart. So I know now that for me to get in school and get my education would be a struggle, but it shouldn't be very much of a problem. Someday I want to be a registered nurse. I don't really want to be a registered nurse, but that right now is on my mind. What I really want to be, I haven't had any foundation on that yet, but I know for starters I would start with being a registered nurse. I always wanted to be a model, you know, I wouldn't mind that. A teacher, I wouldn't mind that, but yet the money is not too good these days. And that's another thing, being in things for money is not good, 'cause your heart is not in it. You got to be in it with your heart. But I don't think I would be a teacher, because the money wouldn't be good so my heart wouldn't be in it. I wanted to be an architectural engineer when I was little, but I don't know now. I really don't know— it's between a registered nurse, a model, and a social worker. I want to work with kids.

I would love to go to college. Yeah, I am supposed to be going to get my GED. So once I finish the GED program I'll have twenty-four college credits. I was accepted into a program that helps you prepare for college. I went to the place, right, and I had to cheat on the test. Not cheat, but I had to make the grade lower, make my grade lower just to get in. Because the program is so good, but they only take you if you got between a fourth, and eighth, grade reading level. And I looked at the test and I was one of the first, as a matter of fact, I was the first person to finish. I talked to them the other day and they told me I could still start the program. You work one week and you go to school one week. The work program pays you $117 and the school program pays you $48. But then where I am living, you know, my rent and the car fare and everything, I wouldn't be able to handle that because the money wouldn't be enough, so I left that.

My family, I don't even like to deal with them. I more or less stay away from my family. I go to my mother's house every weekend to see my son, who is four years old now. That is the only reason I put up with it. But when I go over to her house, if her room is messed up, she says, "Oh, you see what your son did." I'd say, "You and your husband sleep in this room. And even if my son did come in there and mess it up, you let him do that. That's not my fault."

I don't necessarily see myself having a family someday. If I could have all boys I would have as many as I can make. I'm serious. I wouldn't want to have girls. Well, first of all, I wouldn't want her to be like me, okay, because I can be hell at times. I wouldn't want her to be like me. I wouldn't want her to experience the things that I have been through. I just love boys; if I could have fourteen boys I would and my last child I would have a girl, and then I would appreciate her more. And I would also have a lot more experience. But right now I am not thinking about having kids.

I do have a boyfriend now—he's nice, you know, he sees to it that I am okay, that I am never without. I don't see him very often, because, you know, being that I work, I don't like to see my boyfriend every day. Oh, God, I hate that. I get so tired of looking at them. I prefer, like, if it was up to me it would be like on a Saturday and that's it. But I see him maybe twice, three times a week. He works from eight to five and then he goes home and if he doesn't go home that is his business. You know I really could care less because I am not in love with him. I am not looking for a relationship, and I have a very big fear of AIDS, so I make sure that protection plays a very big part in that. I am not as sexually active as I would like to be, but then I don't mind that sacrifice because at least I don't have to worry about having AIDS, or herpes, or VD, for that matter, or anything. I don't need any of that, I don't need it. So, I am not looking for love, you know, I am just looking for somebody to keep me from being lonely. I know my boyfriend cares about me, I wouldn't exactly say that he loves me, although he tells me that, but I wouldn't exactly say he loves me. My boyfriend is going to buy me an engagement ring next week. Of course I am going to accept it but I am not going to marry him. He'll be twenty-one. But, he is a very stupid guy. Believe me, you all may think I'm wrong, even Patty and Sheila told me this, but anybody who is that stupid deserves to be taken advantage of. I'm sorry, that's just how I feel; if you're that stupid you need to be taken advantage of. At least the next girl you won't let her take advantage of you like that. Don't men take advantage of us?

I feel pretty good about myself now. 'Cause I know I have been through a lot and I am still here, and I am not on drugs anymore, and I love God so much more. My mother, she doesn't look at me like the way she used to. When I was on drugs, she knew. I am the kind of person that you can tell when I am doing real bad. I am not doing that great right now, as far as my financial situation, but I am content. I wouldn't say happy, but I am satisfied, and that is all I ever wanted to be is satisfied. Right now I am satisfied. I used to hate my job but now, I look forward to going to work because we have a new general manager and he cares. He shows that he cares. So right now I'm pretty much okay. But I can't complain. I am trying to stop smoking, I'm like a chain-smoker.

I see my son every weekend. I can see him more than that if I was to go over there, but, you know, with me working, then I'll be going to school. So the weekend is about the best I can do right now. My son, I don't know, I believe if I don't take him, that he won't lead the same kind of life that I did. You know, my mother may never put him out but he may be just as bad as me. I wasn't bad, I was just a victim. I always felt that the things I am going through now—God is putting me through these things. I don't want to be rich, I want to be comfortable . . . so when I finally do become comfortable, you know, God is going to be right. What you went through, you know the bad times, you know the good times, you know the difference between right and wrong. This is yours, you worked hard for it. I don't want to wake up one morning and have a house and a car, and not have to pay any mortgage and light bills, or nothing like that. I want to work for it, I want to work to earn my house. So when I do have the house I can say, "Look, I worked for it, I worked hard, it's mine and I'm going to take care of it." But I'm willing to admit that I'm the kind of person, if you give me something, I won't take care of it. I mean, if my boyfriend gives me this shirt, then I won't take care of it as if I had bought it myself. You know, if something happens to it, I say, "Oh, well, I didn't buy it, what the hell." But if I had bought it myself, oh, boy, I have a fit. You know. So I don't want anything handed to me. I want to work for it and I want to see to it that God sees that I'm healthy enough to work for it, and that when I get it I can be thankful. I don't want to be where, when I finally come to it, I don't want to say, "Well, it's about time." I don't want to be like that. I just want to say, "Thank God," because I worked hard enough for it and I believe I deserve it. That's the way I want it to be.

Carrie
(twenty-three years old)

I was two years old when my parents brought me up north. We had been living down south in Georgia, which is where my mother's family is from. The only thing my parents really told me about how I was when I was real little was that they used to let me play on the front porch and I used to take off my diaper and run around naked and the neighbors used to walk by and yell silly remarks at me. That's the only thing I remember. My mother was twenty-one and my father was twenty-four when I was born. My father was working in a factory, and I guess my mother stayed home, she never said.

I don't know why we moved up here . . . I don't remember much about my early years. I didn't go to kindergarten . . . stayed home until first grade. There was this little boy that I liked, I remember him, in first grade. I always liked school. I don't remember too much about it. Probably those years weren't so happy, because if they were happy I would be able to remember them.

Things aren't really too clear in my mind until I was ten years old. Before that, I don't know. Then I remember a lot of beatings and that I couldn't have friends over. We were told that we weren't good enough . . . my father told us we weren't good enough to have friends over. My parents never had company over.

I have one older brother, John, and three other siblings: Patty is twenty-two, Jean is nineteen, and Earl is seventeen. I was pretty close with Jean and Earl, but not Patty . . . she is a miss goody-two-shoes. Except for Patty, all of us kids have run away from home.

I don't remember whether I got beat before I was ten. I remember when my brother got sent away to a treatment center, because we used to go visit him. He's an arsonist and he robbed people. He got out a couple of years later, but then he burnt down a church for my father. I have no idea, to this day I have no idea why my father wanted that church burnt down. But he paid my brother and a couple of other guys fifty dollars each to burn down the church and my brother took the blame for it.

Then they sent him away to some other place, and when he got out he came back home and my father kicked him out. Then he took to the streets, and today he's in prison.

So it was right around when my brother first got sent away that I remember the beatings. My father would come home in a bad mood and he would take it out on everybody, even my mother. He beat us all up. He'd hit us with his fists and also with belts. He hit us anywhere he could, but was pretty good about making sure that he didn't leave bruises or welts visible on our bodies. He didn't drink much, it's not like he had to be drunk to beat us up, but if he had a bad day he would come home and beat us up. He would beat us up about four or five times a week. He scared me for a long time, a couple of years; I just silently lived with it. Then it just made me pissed off and I decided I had had enough. My mom was real scared of him and she'd do whatever he said.

Well, I went to Catholic schools and when I was about thirteen, they had this thing called "grub day" where you could wear whatever you wanted to. Well, I had bought a brand new pair of jeans, the first pair of jeans I had ever owned, and I put on a nice blouse and jeans and I was gonna go to school. But my father said there's no way, he was not going to let me go out like that and told me to put on my school uniform. He told me to get upstairs and change out of my jeans or he would take them off me. So I went upstairs and I sat on my bed waiting for him to come up and sure enough he did, and he started to rip my jeans. He had a pair of scissors and cut and ripped them. And I swung at him and I hit him and he yelled for my mother and he took off his belt and he and my mother were holding me down. I picked up my heavy work boots and I hit my mother with them in the head so that she would let go of me. Then I bit my father and left. I went to school, but when I went home I got my ass whipped. I knew that was going to happen, but I had no place else to go. I mean, I didn't have very many friends. That night after I got home, I got my ass whipped, I was sent to my room without dinner and stuff, and they locked the door so that I couldn't get out. Well, my bedroom was on the second floor of the housing project. So after my parents went to bed I left home. I climbed out of the window and went over to my grandmother's house. In her garage was my bicycle which I took and I was gone. I slept on this man's back porch in a housing project. I didn't go to school during this time, 'cause I knew that would be the first place they would look for me. Besides, I had some money in the bank. Every Tuesday he put a couple of dollars in the bank; I had four-hundred dollars in the bank, so I was going to get that. I saw my parents standing outside the bank waiting for me; I said, well, I guess I won't go get that money. This guy was actually a friend of my father's. But I trusted him, that he wasn't going to tell on me. His wife made me dinners. They knew what was going on, I had told them. His wife wouldn't let me sleep in the house, though, so he gave me a sleeping bag and some blankets and pillows.

I stayed on and off there for most of the summer. It was just before school started because I turned myself in to the department of Social Services the first day of school, so I could go to school. I wanted to go to school. I told them there was no way I was going home, and if they sent me back home I would just leave again. Then, I was placed in a temporary foster home. They did an investigation and we had to go to court. I don't remember what the outcome of the investigation was. All I know is that I didn't have to go back home. I was thirteen years old and they placed me in a temporary foster home.

My foster parents were pretty good, they were pretty cool, but they were only a temporary foster home. I was there for about six months and then they stuck me in another foster home, but I was taken out of there when I tried to break a girl's ribs.

Right around that time, I started hanging out with people since I wasn't home, and I started hanging out with some of the wrong friends. We got caught rolling reefer in the cafeteria by the principal, and the girl that I was caught with was kind of a troublemaker and they expelled her. I thought that they were going to do the same to me so I threatened to kill her. Well, I found out later that they just were going to suspend me, but then they expelled me because I threatened her. I was in tenth grade. So they kicked me out of school and put me in another foster home which I didn't like at all. They didn't pay much attention to me, they had a whole bunch of kids. This one girl who was their real daughter broke one of my Elvis Presley albums; I had all of them, the whole collection, and I was pretty pissed off. She got mad because I wouldn't get up and go to school. They had stuck me out there in a school which I didn't like and didn't want to go to. It was just a public school and I wasn't used to public school; you know, being in a Catholic school you act one way. But I kicked her in the ribs, and when she fell down I just kept on kicking her and kicking her. They called my foster home worker and she came out and got me and took me to a girls' group home. I was fourteen years old.

I stayed at that group home for a while, for about a year, until I turned fifteen—it wasn't too bad. During that time I had very little contact with my parents. Right after I went to my first foster home, my parents brought all my stuff up to me and threw it in the front yard. My bed and everything—they just threw it all in the front yard and left. They never called, never tried to reach me. I didn't give a shit. But when I got to the group home, the staff tried to get me back in touch with my parents. One of my counselors and my parents had a little meeting. Those meetings were not too helpful; we did a lot of arguing, always arguing. They were trying to arrange weekend visits at home. I remember going home one weekend. I don't know if I went home before that visit or not. I went home on the weekend of my birthday; I remember that, my fifteenth birthday. That didn't go too well, and I left the first night I was there. I got into an argument, I don't even remember what about, it was dumb though . . . Yeah, I do; I got sunburned, they were barbecuing. I layed down in the sun; if I lay down ten minutes in the sun and I don't move, I'll burn. I told my mom, don't let me go to sleep, and she said okay. Well, she let me go to sleep, she let me sleep for an hour and a half. The whole back of me burned, and I was pretty pissed off.

They took me out of the group home 'cause I got caught leaving the house in the middle of the night with another girl. We left in the middle of the night and went downtown to the south side to get fried chicken and came back. I got caught and kicked out. Then they stuck me in another temporary foster home, but I ran away as soon as they put me there. I didn't want to be in foster care anymore. Screw it, I wanted to be on my own.

The next thing I did was move into the YWCA. I just went there; I wasn't going to school much, I was skipping a lot. School was a place that I didn't want to be in; the only class that I liked was graphic arts, we did all sorts of printing things. So I moved into the Y, they let me move in with no money. I went down to check out about public assistance because I wasn't sixteen yet, and I couldn't get it. I had to take my parents to court for support and all that other bullshit . . . They told me I couldn't get public assistance until I was sixteen, to begin with, and I said okay. That's when I started pulling tricks and stuff downtown to get money to pay for my room at the Y. When I turned sixteen, I went back to public assistance and I filled out all the papers and garbage, and I had to take my parents to court for support and my father won that case. He said that if I wasn't living at home that he wasn't going to pay support. So, that was just fine and dandy. And the judge in the family court emancipated me so my parents didn't have to pay support.

I was sitting out on this street one night downtown, I was just sitting at the circle, and this guy pulled over and asked me if I wanted to go out. I said, "All right, let's go." So I got in the car and I didn't know what he meant; I thought we were gonna go party. And then I found out what he was talking about. Well, I said, that was easy money, never really got scared, I was very picky. After that night, I was very picky about who I went out with. I only went with older guys; older guys are usually nice. Once in a while I would go out with someone new, very seldom, usually older guys, because they are either married or their wife died. I was pulling tricks on my own, and never worked for anybody. I decided that if I was going to do that kind of stuff, I was going to keep my money. It was interesting, and I met lots of strange people.

I stopped going to school altogether. I hung out at this circle with a whole group of people—everybody was doing it. And that is where I ran into my brother John again. I saw him once at the group home, and he was going to break me out, he said. But the next time I saw him was at the circle and he was doing the same thing that I was doing—pulling tricks.

Nobody at the Y ever questioned me as to how I made my money. As long as my rent was paid, they didn't care. My rent was eighteen dollars a week or something. I always had spending money, though. I would only go out and do tricks one night a week and I'd have a couple hundred dollars on me for the week. I always had new clothes—I was all set. From time to time, I went to Friendship House, a runaway program—I was about sixteen I think when I began doing that. I never lived there—just went there to hang out, just to hang out. I knew a couple of counselors there whom I liked to talk to. They knew what I was up to on the streets and tried talking me out of it and stuff.

I was arrested twice, but I was never convicted of it. I was convicted of loitering once, and the other time was dismissed—there was no real proof that I was doing anything. I was walking down the street and they'd ask if I wanted a ride and I would get in. The first time I was arrested for leaving the scene of an accident, and driving without a license. I had stolen this trick's car. I kicked him out at Riverside Park and drove off, went downtown and picked up a couple of friends, and we went cruising and stuff. I was hiding this one girl in my room at the Y because she had run away from home; she was fourteen or something like that. We drove past her house and her father was sitting on the porch and she yelled "fucking asshole" to him. He followed us in his car and started chasing us. So I am riding around on the West Side going 100–105 miles an hour, and this was the first time I had ever even driven a car. I was just cruising, and the cops were following him and I smashed into the back end of a parked car. Everybody got out and started to run. Well, I was caught along with the other guy who was with us, but the girl who was running from her father got away. They put us in the back of the cop car and this girl's father came over and looked in the car, and he told the cops that I wasn't her but I was in the car. Well, I went to jail because I told them that I was the driver, and I went to jail. In the morning I got out; I was released on my own recognizance. I was sixteen at the time. I went back to the Y to take a shower and everybody was saying, "I thought you were in jail," and I said, "How did you find out?" and they said "Helene told us." Helene, huh, all right. That was the girl who had seen me. I confronted her about it and asked her whether she told everyone that I had been arrested. "No, I didn't tell nobody." Fine. So I went to my room and took a shower and got cleaned up, and as I was leaving one of the counselors asked me about jail and I said, "How did you find out?" "Oh, Helene told us." So I said, "She did, did she?" So I saw her in the elevator when I was going back downstairs to go out and I asked her about it again and she said no, so I punched her in the face. I got kicked out of the Y for that. And so they had taken me upstairs and told me to get all of my stuff because I was leaving. Helene was sitting downstairs. Helene is the one that had seen me get arrested. Okay? I beat her up on my way out too; she had these clogs on and I took them off and I was beating her and she had me arrested for that but she didn't fight me back, and I made that clear to the judge. He goes, "She didn't fight back?" She was sitting in the courtroom and they asked her about it and she said, no, she didn't, she was afraid. And the judge says, well, if she didn't want to fight back there was no sense of pressing charges, and he dismissed the case.

So after I got kicked out of the Y, I moved into this house on Grant Street. I knew one girl who was living there, and I didn't know it but it was like a whorehouse. He'd rent rooms out and most of the girls who hung out there were either junkies or whores. He wasn't actually a pimp, he had a couple of extra rooms there. I lived there for a long time, for a couple of years, until I was eighteen. During that time, I was getting public assistance, because I started getting that when I was at the Y. But I also had the extra money from doing the tricks. I was doing pretty well. I was drinking every night. I got to where I was pulling tricks every night. And I was doing a lot of drinking . . . I used to drink a fifth of Southern Comfort a day. I started probably about nine o'clock at night and I'd continue until I passed out. Then I would sleep most of the morning away. Get up, get ready to go out, and pull some tricks and go out drinking after that. I did a lot of T's and B's (speed)—I did them for a while. I was doing a lot of drinking, a lot of drinking; I used to smoke reefer a lot then too. I can't stand reefer anymore.

I started getting sick of this life-style after I met Sue. I was still going to counseling and it was when I was living on Grant Street. I continued pulling tricks for a while because Sue was doing it too . . . Sue is the girl I live with now. I am gay now, and me and Sue are in a relationship. I was seventeen, because I was still jailbait when I met Sue. She was pulling tricks at that time. We met when the state fair was in town that year back in '81 and became friends. She's from Tennessee and had a boyfriend at the time and was bisexual. She and her boyfriend got in trouble with the law down in Tennessee and they ran. We had gotten jobs at the state fair and we just decided to stay with the fair and travel a little bit. Even though we were making a lot less money working for the fair, it was neat. You know, run away with the circus. I was doing a toss game. It was pretty dumb, but I liked it all right. When the state fair left, I left with one part of the fair and she left with the other. She went to Connecticut and I went to Maryland. We had plans to meet in Charlotte, where the two parts were to meet up.

I liked working for the fair, but it didn't last for very long. I soon came back home. I left and called an old trick who came down to Maryland to pick me up and bring me back. I knew Sue was still in Connecticut. So after I came back home I was still getting my public assistance checks. I straightened a few things out and then I left for Connecticut where I hopefully was going to meet up with Sue. I just thought I would go up there and be with her for a while. But when I got there I learned that she had left there too. I had no idea where she had gone, so I turned around and I hitchhiked back to here again. And I stayed around at Grant Street. Sue wasn't around nowhere. But then I received a Christmas card from her in December. She had gone back home and she and her boyfriend had turned themselves in. Her daddy bought her way out of trouble, but her boyfriend's father wouldn't do it for him, so he was sentenced to forty-five years in prison. That's a pretty stiff sentence; they are really strict down in Tennessee, you can get up to five years for stealing a bicycle. They robbed a drugstore with a gun. They were into drugs real bad, I mean worse than I had ever seen anybody. They did anything they could get their hands on. Anything. Her boyfriend ended up getting killed in prison.

Before I had heard from Sue I had moved out of Grant Street and moved into an apartment on Langer Street, my own apartment, about three or four blocks away. I had gotten enough public assistance to pay all the rent and the heat bill and stuff, and they gave me food stamps for food and stuff, so any money I made on the streets was mine. So I started cutting back on pulling tricks and I had stopped using the T's and B's so much. I don't know, I guess I had enough. So I slowly decreased everything.

And then one night I started hanging out with this one girl, her name was Donna, and she got me in trouble. I didn't know she was going to rob this guy at first. She told me he was her grandfather and when she called him grandpa and everything, he answered. We went to his house and he had just gotten his Social Security check. She sprayed furniture polish in his eyes and took his money and I took the car to get away. I was kind of like an innocent bystander, but I was arrested for robbing him, not stealing his car, because I was there. We had gotten several blocks away and I parked the car and left the keys in the car and walked back downtown. I told her that she could do whatever she wanted to with that money; it was her money and I didn't want to know what she did with it. I helped her to get away . . . I was walking down this street downtown and the cops asked me to come here, and I figured, well, they know I did something; I'm going to be in trouble, but if I lie it will only make it worse. So I went over to the cop car and he asked me to get in. I got in the back and he told me that I had robbed somebody, and they brought the guy down to identify me and he had known who I was. I went to jail for robbery of the second degree. I was there for about a week. I wasn't quite eighteen and it was an adult jail. I knew a lot of the people there, since a lot of them hung out downtown. It didn't scare me, not really. Then I was released on my own recognizance after about a week and I went back and forth to court for about a month. I was given five years probation and had to report in once a week or once every two weeks. I didn't like that very much, I didn't like probation. My probation officer kept violating me, over and over and over for nitpicky things. Whenever I was put on probation I was told I couldn't drink, so I cut down a lot. I was still pulling tricks, but I just didn't tell her.

After I got the card from Sue, I wrote her back a letter and she wrote me and we wrote letters for a couple of months, and then I wanted to move out of my apartment and move into a better place. Well, I moved back with my foster parent, Wilma Taylor. We kept in touch and every now and then I would call her all through this time. Well, she rented me a room for twenty dollars a week for room and board.

I moved in and Wilma let me use the phone to call Sue in Tennessee and stuff as long as I paid for the phone calls, so I said, no problem. I stopped turning tricks and everything; I kind of cut them off because I was getting welfare. We told Welfare that I was paying more money for rent than I really was, so I got more money. She was pretty understanding and wanted to get me off the streets. I think that is why she offered to let me move in. So I moved in there and I paid for the phone calls and stuff.

I knew I wanted to be with Sue; I wasn't sure what she wanted. We had slept together twice the whole time we had known each other. I had never really been with another woman before, but I wanted to find out what it was about. When I was in the group home, they had a big brother, big sister program. I had a big sister and she was gay. I didn't find out until I was living at the YWCA and she had come to see me one day. She had offered to let me move in with her and I was going to. We were sitting in Burger King and she said, "Well, I have something to tell you before you move in with me." And I was, like, all right. I just looked at her and she said, "Maybe I shouldn't tell you," I said, "Just tell me, I hate when people do that shit to me." And she goes, "All right," and I was taking a bite out of my cheeseburger, she said, "I'm gay." I was, like, okay, so, I was just watching her and she said, "That doesn't bother you?" I was, like, no. It was, like, strange, I had never realized, I never thought about it, and it was amazing how many of my friends are bisexual that I didn't know about. Then I learned a lot more of my friends were gay than I knew. So it interested me and I was curious. I found it more enjoyable than being with a man. I really never had a boyfriend. Right after I first left home there was a guy that I had a relationship with, but he was a friend of my brother and he had been in and out of jail. The group home didn't think it was a good idea for me to see him, you know. After he went to jail once I just kind of lost interest for a while. Then there were guys that I went out with that I wouldn't get paid for, but nothing real serious.

After I moved back in with Wilma, I hadn't turned eighteen yet. When I was living with Wilma I got off welfare, and I got a job folding diapers at a diaper service. I opened up a bank account and everything, and saved up enough money to bring Sue here to visit me for two weeks, for a hotel for us and everything. She was living in Tennessee with her son Matthew and she was living on welfare. I bought her a bus ticket. I had to be at work the morning she arrived so I picked her up at the bus station and brought her up to the hotel and put her and Matthew in bed to sleep, they had been traveling all night, and then I went to work. When I came back I woke them up. They had slept a good ten hours when I was gone. Sue stayed here for two weeks and then decided to go back. I went back with her, even though I was on probation at that time, I was violating my probation. Well, my probation officer at that time was pretty nice and she had contacted Wilma. The morning we went I quit my job. I don't know how Wilma felt about this, I don't know, I didn't really ask her. I didn't take much stuff of my own, just a couple sets of clothes, and I was gone. And we went down to Tennessee to where she was living and I stayed there from March to June, the beginning of June, because it was after my birthday. She stayed down there for about two more weeks. Back up north, I moved in with some guy I knew from Grant Street and talked him into going and getting Sue for me since he had a truck.

Well, we had to come back here because of my probation. So I rode down there with him, and Sue didn't believe that we were coming to get her, and she told me on the phone that she had packed everything up and she was just waiting. We got down there and nothing was packed. So, it took us an hour to just throw everything in the back of the truck and came up here and we stayed there at that house for a couple of months until she got on welfare and then we found an apartment here in the city and we have lived here pretty much since then. We've had our fights now and then, and I would have a little fling here and there, but we've been together now for about five and a half years.

We moved into this place and both were on welfare. We didn't get jobs for a long time; she hasn't had a job since she lived here. We both stopped pulling tricks entirely, not too long after that, like a couple of months after. And I stopped getting high and stopped doing T's and B's;

still drank now and then, not very much. Sue continued to drink and she got high once in a while. We decided we were going to start right. Then we decided to have a kid together, but since there was no way I could get her pregnant, the closest thing to me was my brother. Well, he'd do anything to get laid, so we fixed it up so that we got him to move in with us and I got pissed off and I moved out. This was a plan, so I moved out and rented a little hotel room downtown and then Sue and him slept together once. It only took once, and she got pregnant. Then, I moved back in and kicked him out.

I've sanded off most of my tattoos. I did them myself. I did them way back when I was living at the group home. There was one time when me and Sue got into a fight and I met this girl. She wasn't gay then but she is now. To this day she still is gay because she calls me every now and then at work. Anyway, I had tattooed her name in my arm and her nickname, and, well, Sue didn't like that. Then there was another time I got into a fight and I tattooed BETSY down by my wrist, and LYNN across the middle of my arm—she was my big sister at another group home. I had about six tattoos. I sanded them all off with sandpaper except one. Eventually I'll do that one too, and even though my arm has these red areas it's gonna clear up.

I have had a few jobs. I got a job at a pizzeria and I worked there for a few months and then I got tired of it. So I quit, then I got a job driving a school car for about six months and then I went to work for my boss. He had a partner who also owned a moving business. I didn't actually quit, I just kind of transferred over for a while. Then I got into a car accident while I was working and totaled the car. I had hurt my back, I was on my back for a couple of months, no biggy. Sue took care of me. Then after that, the delivery service had gone out of business, so what I did was I went down and I got my taxi license and I started driving that. I did that for a couple of months. Sue didn't like that because I was driving from six at night to six in the morning. She didn't like that because of the weirdos out at night and stuff, and so I quit that and I went to work for an old trick—he owns a business uptown—and I learned how to operate large machines at a factory and I kept his books for him. Then his business started slowing down so he just laid me off, and while I was laid off I got this job down here at the paper mill. In May it will be two years since I have been there.

Sue is on welfare. We made it all legal; they take a certain amount of money out of her for me because we stated that I give her money for rent. My whole paycheck, everything, goes into the house. Shannon is my kid too. He knows that Sue and I are gay and he knows what is going on and he is accepting that. I never thought that I would be a parent. In my house there is no more hitting, I mean like spanking their butt—we don't do that anymore. For some time, we used to spank them. Then it got to the point where they would just laugh at you so we decided there would be no more hitting in our house and that we would punish them in other ways. If they throw a toy the toy is gone; we tell them that we throw them away. We have this closet full of toys. One of these days we are going to have to let them have them. If they're just running through the house being loud—because we have older people who live downstairs from us and they are on oxygen tanks and stuff, so there is no running and stuff. If they run they have to sit in—we have this chair in the corner and it is called the bad chair and they have to sit in the bad chair for five minutes. And Matthew hates the bad chair because your time doesn't start until you shut your mouth and you sit there quietly. If you do not sit there right, the time doesn't start until you start sitting there right. So he's been there, the longest I think he has ever been there is about half an hour. And it is like, would you just give me a whooping so I can go play. He doesn't want the chair. Shannon will sit there like a trooper. And then he'll get up and be good for a while. We have a bad chair but no hitting.

I guess what has helped me to survive all these experiences is people. My counselor at the group home is number one and was always there for me to talk to. She was successful, and she had a job, and I wanted to grow up and be like her.

I am a survivor. I do what I have to do. Other people who helped me along the way were my foster parent, Wilma Taylor—she was okay, she was nice, and if I needed a place to stay I could always go there. She was more of a family to me than my parents. I mean I have to admit that. Yeah, she was like a family to me. At one time I just decided it was time to grow up and stop messing around. And so I did.

I just survived. You know kids, they just get to a certain point, like my brother, he got to a certain point I think he enjoys jail now because he is in and out of there so many times. I think, my parents might have had an influence on my surviving. They always told me I would be like him, so I was like, I will show you . . . I haven't seen them in a couple of years now, but my brothers and sisters see them and they tell them what I am up to. I see Jean and Earl, and Patty lives around the corner from me, she comes over every now and then.

In five years, hopefully I will be going to school, to college, because by then Shannon will be in school full-time and Sue will be able to go to work or whatever she wants to do. For now, hopefully, we are going to start looking in June for a place further out of the city, like in the country. Probably an apartment.

I don't think I would have changed anything about my past—not even my parents. If it wasn't for my parents hitting on me and stuff I would have never moved out or done all this other stuff. I could have lived home until I was married, like my little sister Patty.

I used to cry when we got snow days because I wanted to go to school. I got my GED in 1983 and I've gone to college for criminal justice, I have gone through two semesters for criminal justice because I wanted . . . someday I want to become a lawyer. At the present moment I don't have any plans. One of these days I am sure I will just get tired of working and go to school again. One of these days I am going to become a lawyer. But I am happy right now, stable . . . I'm definitely in control. I'd like to be a criminal lawyer, and I want to work with kids. I would like to defend kids, because I feel some of them get bad deals . . . like me.

Chuck
(seventeen years old)

I was born on June 30, 1970. My mom, she was working in a factory. She had just moved here and she was in her early twenties. She already had three children. I was the fourth. She had two when she left down south, then she moved up here, then she had my sister about a year and a half before she had me. I know my sister is from the same father but I don't know about the other two.

All I know about my father is that he was young, he couldn't hold a job, and the marriage was breaking up. He was always drinking and all kinds of stuff like that. Mom doesn't talk about him much, and when anybody does she gets mad. I guess he wasn't that great a guy. He disappeared after I was born. As a matter of fact he claimed I wasn't his. He just, you know, floated off into the sunset.

I never had any contact with him until recently. I think he even lived with us a little while. I seen some pictures one time, a lot of pictures of him with my sister. But I never seen pictures of him with me when I was really little. I discovered some cousins of his that lived here. His cousin has some kids and they live here and I met up with them a couple of years ago. I got a lot of information about my father through them. I saw him a couple of times. He didn't even know who I was at first. I left it that way. When he knew who I was, he didn't, you know . . . I didn't say anything 'cause I knew what it was like. My sister had lived with him and she ran away. She couldn't handle it. So I didn't say nothing to him.

I was wild when I was little. I was very wild. I was very depressed, you know, 'cause, like, Mom started going to college and she married my stepfather when I was four. Then we moved. I don't know when we moved but I remember I was real little. My stepdad's name was Marcus. She married him and I remember, she taught us how to read when we were little. I remember that because I was reading by the time I was like three or four if not earlier She bought us little books, Dr. Seuss type stuff. I got into school early. I used to go to this day care center for a little while. Then we moved again to the area where I live now.

I hated school. I mean I was excited about it, but, I just never liked it. I hated school. My mother, I don't know, she always used to hit us if we did something wrong. But she was abusive in other ways, she used to tease me in front of her friends about my appearance and other things. I wouldn't walk until I was two. I just didn't want to walk, you know, and she used to curse me out. She wanted me to walk bad, and I didn't want to do it, I was lazy, I didn't feel like walking. And like one time I remember, it was like my aunt and one of my aunt's friends and my mother and my stepfather or maybe my real father, something like that, they was all around me. They were just getting on my case about walking. And finally, I got up and I walked, you know, and then everybody left me alone for a little while. It was little stuff like that, that I remember.

They used to get on my case about all kinds of stuff. Even my sister was on my case all the time. Like when I was in school or when I was away from home, I would just break loose and act stupid or something. Oh, yeah, there was something else, we had this baby-sitter who used to do us wrong. I forgot what her name was. My mother didn't like using baby-sitters, but she used one when she started going to school. Now, I remember this baby-sitter did something to us and my mother stopped using baby-sitters. The baby-sitter would never watch us and I think my sister hurt her head or something. She used to strap me in a car seat and leave me somewhere. One time my mom came home and my sister had hurt herself and the baby-sitter was on the phone and I remember a whole big scene. After that she started taking us to college with her. We would sit down and answer questions. She would make us pay attention and, you know, she made us write down stuff and all that. She just made us sit down and my brothers were really answering questions. It was crazy.

One day I was looking through Mom's room and I found a manuscript she had written. I learned a lot of stuff about what happened. I found out that my sister was taken away from her when she was two and that began the whole big foster care thing. I wasn't in foster care until I was about twelve. My sister was in and out of foster care from the time she was two because my mother used to beat her.

My real father wanted to take my sister, but my mother wouldn't go for it. So CPS came in and took my sister for a while. Then they brought her back and all kinds of garbage was going on. I remember when I was like six or seven she was gone. When she was eight they took her away for a long time. I didn't like that, man, I was crazy. My sister was in and out of foster care running away from all this.

When it came to my mother beating us—we all got the same treatment. She was equal, if she beat one she would beat the other one. For whatever reason, you know, if I did anything wrong or not she was very equal. She was just very, very young. In her book she wrote a lot about what she did when she was young and that helped me to see why she was so hard on us. She did some really crazy stuff when she was young, like she had four kids before she was twenty-one, you know, so, like, you know, she was just determined not to let it happen to us, I guess. She tried to make something better of herself, but at the same time she wasn't ready to have kids. That's the bottom line, she wasn't ready and she really couldn't handle them. She can't handle stress as it is. So with a couple of kids running around, that was just enough to make her crazy. I guess it was just stress or it was just not being able to deal with everything. There were a lot of reasons why she beat us; I can't put a finger on it but I guess she was really strict because she didn't want the same things to happen to us that happened to her. That's why she was so, so strict. Very strict.

I'm not really sure what it was with my sister, but all I know is in later years I realized how much they were alike. They were almost twins, they were so much alike. I guess that must have bummed my mother out totally 'cause she could see herself in this kid and that's the reason why she was so harsh on her and kind of lax on me. I know we used to visit her in the foster home. My mother used to take us all the time, and I remember that when she came back from the foster home she was talking about how good it was over there and how bad it was at home. I guess when she was, like, nine she started running away.

My mother was always beating us for something. We'd do something stupid, and she used to take us downstairs and tie us to the pole and take a cord and beat us with it. I kind of got used to it, but when it was my sister's turn she just wasn't going for it. One time she just said, "No, you ain't going to do it, this time, it's not going to happen." She was, like, nine years old and she ran upstairs and ran out. I was scared 'cause I'd never seen anyone saying anything like that to my mother. I was like, wow, this kid's got guts. In a little while the police came and brought my sister back and talked to my mother about the beating and whatnot. After that my sister just ran all the time. I remember I ran with her twice. But I wasn't into it, you know, I was very cool about things. They used to beat me and I would just . . . well, I always had somebody to lean on.

My stepfather, he was, like, the cool one, you know. He was always the mediator, trying to calm my mother down. When she would say no he would say yes. That's the reason why their marriage broke up 'cause he was always telling her to cool out and give us a break and that kind of thing. She took our TV from us, like, when we were six. She wouldn't let us watch TV for, like, years. Actually, it did a lot of good for us. I remember I used to see my stepfather reading all the time. I used to make my own toys. I used to be bored and I had a room full of books, and I used to just read a lot. Sometimes my stepfather would let us watch TV when she went to work.

My mom and my stepdad split up after my sister left for the last time.

My sister was, like, fourteen when she left and she never came back. I was probably twelve or thirteen. She was in ninth grade. She got pregnant and she had an abortion. I think somewhere between twelve and fourteen she got pregnant again and she had another abortion. Then when she was fourteen she got pregnant and had the kid. She was in and out of group homes for her running away. I mean the longest she was at home was like two years. You know, they'd take her to group homes and she would run from there and all kinds of wild stuff. The funny thing is when we were in school we were always honest injuns, that was the crazy thing. My sister, when she was in school, she was always on the honor roll. She was just out there doing all kinds of crazy stuff and my mother put her in a private school. My mother was beating her at the time and the sisters at the private school started investigating my mother. My mother took her out of the school and put her in middle school for the next year.

My mother had this way of trying to get the whole family to go against each other, you know, she would say to me the reason why you can't go to school is because your sister has messed it up for you. And she would say to my stepfather the reason why she messed up is because you were being too nice to her and, you know, my stepfather would be, like, quit bugging me, get off my case. In the meantime I was always very quiet at home. I rarely spoke out against any abuse at home because my sister was always the voice of power. She raised the roof; I'd just sit back and let her do all the hell raising. My stepfather used to get frustrated and he would beat my mother up and then she would come and beat us up. It was wild.

She would get on his case about being nice to us, you know, and he always tried to state his case. They used to go out and she would make scenes for no reason. He used to get pissed about it and try to speak to her about it calmly but she would blow up. He's normal, a big dude, he doesn't take that from people. He had a lot of problems himself. His family goes into a whole different dimension. He was in 'Nam and when he came back he had three kids of his own.

I tried to have contact with his kids but my mother wouldn't go for it. My stepbrother Craig, he was the middle brother of the three, he would try to be in contact with us. He tried, him and my stepfather kept in contact all the time. He would try to contact us. I think I first met him when I was eleven. I met all three of my stepbrothers, they tell me, when I was very, very young. Both families met. After that my mother said no more, that's it. I never met the other ones until recently. My stepbrother, it was ironic, he came to work at the house where I am staying, by some twist of fate. So we are pretty tight now.

My stepfather was on cocaine when he met my mother and he was just kicking that problem. There was a lot of stress in the family, stress was what we ran on. That's what we had for breakfast, we had stress, lots of stress, we fell with stress, everybody was just bugging out, and like I said my outlet was school. I would go to school and go crazy. I'd go to school and take off my clothes and run down the hall. I used to do all kinds of things. I got skipped up a grade and I used to chase teachers, run out of the room and just start a fight in school for no reason. I used to get kids to fight each other for money and then sit back and watch. I used to do all kinds of stuff.

They gave up trying to control me. I was so smart. They would say, "Look at you getting A's, how can you do this kind of stuff?" I used to bug them out. I used to play head games with them. I have always been a player. I'd do head games on them and they would just leave me alone.

After a while I learned how to mess a social worker up. That's why there were so many of them. Miss Carr, the first one I met, x'd (slang term) my formula and that's why we are such good friends. She was crazier than myself. Anyway, social workers, I went through tons, they used to come talk to me. They would be involved in my sister's abuse and it was weird 'cause my sister was very verbal. She would say, "I'm being abused, help me." I would just sit back and we would go to court and they would ask me how I felt. I didn't want Mom to get on my case so I just lied. My sister would go in there and say I got beat and raise hell and they would be fighting. My sister was something else. Boy, she was . . .

I finished up eighth grade with no sister. That kind of messed me up. After sixth grade I started having bad years. Seventh grade was a very bad year. I failed almost everything and I had to go to summer school for the first time. And then in eighth grade a good year, honor roll, graduated high in the top of the class, and ninth grade was a bad year. Tenth grade was a good year. Eleventh and twelfth grade was unspeakable. I was doing all kinds of stuff. I just totally gave up by eleventh grade—I was, like, forget it all, I've had enough. Like, um, after my sister left—she was my main source of comfort; when she was around I could talk to her and she was very radical. I didn't realize what a radical was then, but I know now she was. I always admired her ability to stand up to my mother. My stepfather wouldn't even do it. Sometimes he would be, like, forget it, just leave her alone, let her have her tantrum. My sister would be cussin' my mom out. I used to bug out and when she was gone that's when I had to learn how to do that myself.

Around this time there were a lot of violent fights between my mom and my stepfather. He would leave for a month and a half and come back, you know, begging and pleading. There was a lot of garbage for about a year. I think it lasted about a year after that and then he stopped. He just quit. Then it was just me and Mom. That's when it all just blew up. That's when I started realizing it was time to be radical. There was no buffers, no mediators; it was her against me. One of us was going to have to go soon, and I decided I will stay as long as I can. My mother used to do her little tricks on me, she had ways of messing with me. She'd do things, I can't even remember what, I try and block them out now, 'cause she'd just do incredible things to me. And I would do incredible things to mess with her. She had all kinds of devices that were making me crazy. Eventually I just got tired and I started doing devious little things to mess with her. I went from being good and kind, you know, to messing up all the time. That's when I stopped going to school, you know, 'cause I realized school was really important to her and I was, like, well, what better way to mess her up than not go to school.

In school I always had a lot of friends, so by eleventh grade I had some teachers in my pocket. I would go to one class and show all day, you know, max out, help him out, and never go to any other class. Then there was a system that even if you didn't attend the class, if you passed one test at the end of the year you'd pass. Like a regents class, you'd pass at the end of the year. I'd cut school all year, take the exam, and move on. That was my system. I'd go to school and I'd go to class maybe out of a year a hundred days or something, I don't know how many days. Of all the days of school I guess I went for maybe a total of two months was the most time I spent in school. I started doing this when I was in eleventh grade. I used to go and then not go. The second half of eleventh grade I just totaled high school, I said fuck it. I just didn't bother. I just stopped going to class. I failed pathetically for the whole year. But by the end of the year I would somehow get a couple of credits and move on. This is what I'd do.

I met a teacher, he was like an acting instructor and it was with him I really started to discover a lot of things I could do, you know. I never knew I could act so when I met him he was a very radical dude himself. Very liberal, very nonconformist, very laid back. I wasn't used to that. I was used to, you know, stick with the rules, so when I met him I was, like, wow, this dude is really cool. His name is Damien. He was a really cool guy and everybody in the program was like me. They all came from something, and they were all there for something. All of us were good actors or good singers or performers or good technicians or whatever. So we all made up the drama department but for some reason all of us came from a family where there was something going on so I didn't feel so alone. I could go in there with them and we'd talk about our problems. We'd tease each other, you know, it was like one big family down there, and we were in the theater which was in a building separate from the school. We could hide from the rest of the school for the whole day, just be a family, and it was wild. I'd never had one like this and I was in heaven. I'd go in there and chill out all day and that's when I started all my craziness, you know, wearing mismatched sneakers, and that's when "me" came out. That's when I discovered a little bit more about myself. I wasn't so high from the world but I got very, very liberal, very laid back, very up yours. I got very, very, very radical. I thought of doing all kinds of stuff, you know. My mother saw that. She was, like, hmm, this is not the obedience that I want, something is wrong here.

That's when I went to the first foster home. It was supposed to be kind of a placement for a little while to give me time away from my mother but, you know, I ran away from this home and went back to my house. I remember that. That was crazy. It was worse there than it was at my house. CPS is, like, this doesn't make any sense; we take the kid out of his house and he runs back. What is this? That was really crazy. I remember I went back and, like, I can remember like three times, I think it was like three or four times I was taken out of the home for some reason or another. I remember one time I did leave, and I was placed somewhere and sure enough they were giving drugs and I said bye and I went home. Yeah, that was the one, I was about twelve or thirteen, something like that.

I remember one time I was placed somewhere and I had to sleep with this dude and something happened, and I started bugging out. When I got back home I was, like, doing some very strange things because I had this personal thing with sexuality, you know. Sex was not really a big thing with me—well, that's a lie, I was always obsessed with sex. I mean I'm being very honest, I've always been into sex. My stepfather used to have these books and magazines and, you know. I was reading everything I could pick up, but I was very quiet about it. I didn't think about it constantly and I never mentioned it to anyone so when this thing happened with this other resident it kind of blew . . . the guy was a girl, you know, and it was kind of weird. I don't know where it was or why I was there but I remember being there for like three days before I got placed at the place where I ran back home. When I got back home after this I was messed up. I never told anybody. I was very quiet about it. But I started doing some very, very strange things. My stepfather noticed I was doing some odd things. I used to steal my sister's and my mother's undergarments and do all kinds of strange things. I was just doing some very, very strange things, even for me. I used to do some crazy stuff but this is very different. This was, like, I was noticeably doing some wild things, so my stepfather asked me about it and I told him some lie and, you know, like, eventually I stopped. I was, like, doing it for a long time, though, like a couple of months. Then I started thinking, What are you doing? and eventually I chilled out, you know.

I know my mother used to suspect but she never knew. Even if she did know she never told me she knew. She was probably too ashamed or too embarrassed or whatever. But she never confronted me with it: "Why are you doing this?" She was never like that, you know, she would always beat around the bush and come at you from your left side. Attack you. If my stepfather had told her what was up—that's probably why she didn't like Damien, my drama teacher. Like right off the bat she didn't . . . well, then again my sister was in that theater program too before she ran away.

When I got involved she had liked him at first, you know, she was glad I was involved in something, you know. Then when I started to deviate and started hanging out there all day and all night, that's when she started going off on her little binge about not liking him.

When I was fifteen CPS got involved again. There was more of the beating and mental abuse kind of stuff, you know. I can't remember exactly how they got involved. They would check on me every now and then and I guess eventually I would just mention this, that, and the other thing and they would take me away or something. It was during my period of my renaissance, when I was, like, coming out, that I started running away. I was like fifteen, sixteen years old. I was like, hey, I don't got to put up with this, you know, if you mess with me I'm steppin', you know. But what it was, you know, I found friends, people I could go see, you know, I could leave home and go chill with somebody, normal people who were like me, you know. Like sometimes I'd go out and I'd come home and the door would be locked. This was when my mother tried to mess with me so, you know, sometimes I would bang on the door and wake her up and she would have a nice excuse to curse me out, you know, and tell me you're always doing something. Well, you know, after a while I was like, come home, the door's locked and fine, I'd go find somewhere else to sleep, you know, I didn't have no problem with it and so this was happening like on and on from the time I was like fifteen.

The door was always open to the house, you know, we used to leave that open for a long time. She'd go to work and leave it open but usually I was home so I never needed the key. But when she wanted to mess with me she locked it. So, I left for the last time last year or earlier this year. She's living alone now. She had a boyfriend every now and then, but they never got along and I remember one time I left and I was gone for like the longest—this was like last year. It was like August of last year and I left for like about a week. And that was like the longest I'd ever been and not come back.

I got back and there was a big song and dance. She had some tears to make it look good and she said, "Okay, look, you can stay but you have to go to school," and I was like okay, fine, I'll go to school, I got no problem with it. I didn't go to school. I started out, I was, like, I'm going to go to school and I'm going to have a good year. Mother was going crazier and crazier. I said, forget school. By that time I couldn't get into school. I mean school was, like, you couldn't sit me in a classroom for a period. It just wasn't worth it. I was like, no, I can't do it. I kind of gave up on school and that was really the main reason why I left. Mother's craziness wasn't that bad.

I got in this car accident with my mother's car. 'Cause I always wanted to drive I was, like, let me drive, I can drive, and so one day we went out. Me and Mom were very cool. The only time we had problems was when I wasn't going to school or wasn't doing what she said or going out or that kind of thing. That's when she'd get mad but there were days when she was cool. So, one day we went out to get something to eat and she was a little tipsy, you know, so I said, "Mom, just let me drive, you might do something." I didn't have a permit or license or anything, but I could drive. I was driving home and when we got to the light I was sitting back, it was a red light and I was about to make a turn, and as I made the turn, this car was coming, so I turned out of his way and I made the turn too sharp. My mother panics and tries to hit the brakes for me and she hits the gas and we went roaring into this metal fence and I almost hit a pole and somehow we managed to get out of that one. The car was wrecked but we were all right. That was the first major thing where it was her against me and I was, like, I wanted to see what happened with it. Now this would come back to haunt me later, like, in June. I never knew this but, you know, she told the police that I was driving the car, very smart, you know. It could have been taken care of, no problem, but instead she told them I was driving, so I got a ticket, you know, and I had to go to court. I got my tie on, suit on, and I'm going to court, and here comes Mother saying, "Where are you going?" I said court. And she said, "No, you're not," and she starts going crazy about me going to court. And so I said fine, fine. She said "I'll handle it." I said great. I laid back and she supposedly handled it. She didn't but I wouldn't find that out until recently. Anyway, that was the first major thing that happened, and in between this time some things happened with me.

I was interested in girls for the first time. I've had some serious problems. I can't even remember about when all my girl problems began. Me and girls are just problems, total problems. You know, ever since I discovered they existed for obvious reasons I've had problems with females. I used to look at a girl and see my mother and get scared and run. So I never really could get into girls. There was this one who I really dug in tenth grade when I met her and I really, really liked her. She was like the first girl who I really, really . . . you know, I was like *wow*. And there was a girl before her. But this chick was very settled, she was very quiet, you know, so liking her wasn't making it because she didn't reciprocate. But again, something in the past would come back to get me later on. See, this kid, I met her in seventh grade, this is Samantha. I met her in seventh grade, I liked her immediately for some reason. I used to go for the underdog, she was kind of, uh . . . no one would give her a second look and I was like, hmm, there might be something here no one else has seen, so I investigated. I used to mess around when she was here, she was very shy and young, so I was like, uh . . . I'll find something bigger and better, you know, and like that was in seventh grade I was messing with her. I messed with her off and on from seventh grade until in tenth grade I met this chick, Tina, and I just like, uh . . . I fell totally in love. I just went crazy, I was bugging, I'd wish it'd been two years later, man, I was buggin'.

It got very interesting. I never could tell how she felt; she'd give me a sign and then she'd turn me off and then she'd give me a sign and turn me off. I even changed a little bit for her; I started wearing clothes, I even combed my hair. I was doing some weird things to try and get this chick, man, I went to church, I mean I'm telling you, she had me going. I am serious, she had me going. To this day I'm not sure what she was doing, I mean she was the first girl to tell me she loved me. And you can't tell me that, no one tells me that, and when they do, I take it very, very seriously.

Tina was in the program. A lot of things happened in that program. We did a lot of talking. Never went out, you know. I used to go to her house and we'd talk and she'd come to my house and we'd talk and then, uh, this again came back to haunt me. Her mother and my mother became very good friends and that came to cause problems. I got kicked out of my house because of their being such good friends. I told the girl something, she told her mother, and she told my mother. I used to steal from my mother regularly, so she actually kicked me out.

I had a legitimate reason, you know, I used to defend myself. I'd say, "Mom, you spend x amount of dollars on cigarettes and x amount of dollars on booze, you spend x amount of dollars on your little drugs; why can't you give me a little bit of money!" So I used to take a little bit, not a lot, but then, after a while I started getting a little extravagant. I went overboard a couple of times. She suspected and I used to think she was dumb. I'd take a couple of dollars, then she'd catch me and I'd be, like, arrest me!! I was doing that for a long time, from like seventeen, I used to steal all the time. She didn't notice it until it was me and her, and then there was not much I could do without being noticed. Like before I'd have somebody to hide behind, I'd have my stepfather at least; now, she was, like, it's you, you know, so that got a little crazy.

That September when school started, the last year of school, the thing with Tina was starting to get a little out of hand. By this time she had played with my mind for a whole year and had me totally messed up but then again there was still Samantha to worry about. I was seeing Samantha too, you know, so those were the only two girls I was really seriously messing with. There was a time when I wouldn't look at a girl, give a girl a second look, but now, man, I have a lot of girlfriends, I have some good friends, you know, a lot of girl friends, a lot of guy friends, I had a lot of people who I knew and it was a very sudden change and like within two years or so, you know, I got very, very popular. I was very loose, you know, I was very open, very liberal, you know.

I guess it was partially from my involvement with Damien 'cause I really admired him because I'd never met a teacher who was so laid back; he would sit with us, curse at us man, kiss us, mess with us. He was like me in that he could put up a nice front, you know. He's very smart, you know, and he seemed to be, you know, very career oriented, he seemed to be able to help me and we got along good together. He was the first teacher who ever really got ahead of me. I went to his class, I passed his class all the time. I'd give him a call over the summer, I mean not like real tight friends, but we were like best buddies, man, you know, I mean I used to hang with him all the time and that blew up this year too. I'm telling you, I've had a great year.

The thing with Tina was starting to fizzle, but we were still like family friends. I would go to her house, talk to her mother. Me and her mother, we got kind of close. Now I started setting my sights on Samantha. I felt like, this is the last year, I've messed me through for like six years. Something's got to happen so that's when I started getting heavily into Samantha. In the meantime, things at home were blowing up 'cause I wasn't going to school. One thing that helped me was rapping. I discovered rapping, like, when I was fifteen. It was something that I could do. I thought of doing rapping with a little group, me and my best friends in a little group. I started writing stuff and when I was in eleventh grade I started really considering making a record or something.

Rap music is really hot. It's black music, very, very urban, very black. Poetry, man, that's really what we do, you know, we do a lot of rapping, and this music wherever you go in a black community you will hear rap music somewhere, guaranteed. That was something I was doing and my mother, she would support me, but she was like, yo, you got to go to school. So, I'm ready to make records and I'm ready to go get big and famous and my mother's saying you ain't doing jack till you go to school. In December we were going to studios and we were set on making a record. That's what was causing the problem. Mother said, "I don't want you to go to the studio any more and I don't want you to rap anymore and I want you to pick up your grades." I wanted to be in a play that year 'cause I had done very well in the play the year before. I got a lot of great reviews, people liked me in the play before. Ironically, it was *Runaways*. I did very well in that and I wanted to continue on. That's when I started thinking about acting. I also write and I have been writing since

God knows when. I was writing all the time, I always write. I just do it naturally, I've always written. Rapping is something I've been into very heavily for a while and acting was something I wanted to do. It didn't really seem important but I was doing a lot of writing, a lot of rapping, a lot of acting. I wasn't doing a whole lot of schoolwork.

I never used writing as an escape until things started getting bad. When things would get really bad, that's when I would write about what was bugging me out. When things would get bad with Tina, I would write. When things would get bad with Mom, I'd write. I would write as an escape and that's when my writing got good, believe it or not. My writing got really good when I was writing about what was messing me up. And that's when I started considering writing as a possible career, and in the meantime I wrote a book here and there. I wrote a couple of movies, all kinds of stuff. I started to make this record, so I'm getting hot, but Mom is again, "No, no, no." So this is where our conflict began; my mother said, "You are not going to rap and live in this house." I'm, like, yes, I am, and if I can't live here, fine, I'd leave and come back in couple of days. This is going on very heavily now between like August and January. Come January everybody's involved because Mother found out that I was hiding at Damien's for all those years. Now he becomes her public enemy number one and she makes a big thing with the school system over Damien, trying to get him fired. She finally put two and two together that his was the only class I was passing. She later tried to insinuate that he made advances 'cause she was so furious with me, that I could have hidden for two years in one man's class and put it over on her. She was very angry, very angry. So her first impulse was to get rid of this man and by this time I was starting to want to get rid of him too because he was doing some things that weren't too cool to me, you know what I'm saying.

I realized he wasn't what I thought he was. He'll get something from you, give you a little bit of this, and send you walking. If you're not doing anything for him he doesn't want anything to do with you. I was doing everything for him. I was writing a lot of parts to his shows and I was helping him direct. When I stopped doing it, I suddenly became unwanted. It was starting to blow up in my face. Everything was really dim crazy, you know, and I managed to make it to seventeen. I didn't think I'd make it.

I was living at home off and on now. I had a lot of close friends I could stay with, but it wasn't until I got kicked out permanently that I imposed upon them. Sometimes I'd go to Tina's house. That was obviously the first choice. Then sometimes I would just sleep outside somewhere. I'd sleep on the back porch or something. I'd be nearby. I'd never go very far, 'cause I was always a homebody, I didn't want to go away.

I still want to go home but I've been gone so long I'm not even sure what it looks like anymore, and you know, around this time I got to be seventeen. I couldn't believe it, I was, like, wow . . . a milestone, I didn't think I'd make it 'cause I was very suicidal from the time I was like nine. I was fascinated by suicide as well as sex. Suicide was a very good opportunity. I'd get a lot of attention. All I had to do is say I'm going to jump and people would come. I liked that. I'd do that sometimes and I got off on that. Sometimes I just wanted to see what they would do and sometimes I was really ready to end it all. Once, I got really bold and actually shot at something. Once, I think I was like eleven or twelve, I took a whole bottle of vitamins, just to do it. You know, and nothing happened, I was so upset, I was frustrated. My stepfather knew I did that because I told him. He beat me afterwards. He said, "Don't do that." As much as I would think about it, as much as I would want to die, what was going through me was that I could never do it. I'm just soft. I couldn't do that, it just wasn't in me to just end it all. It was an attention-getting thing on and off until the really bad times early last year. By this time I had a couple more suicide tries and didn't make it. I figured I've had enough, I'd just try to do myself in in all kinds of ways.

I'd get into trouble on purpose and get beat down and all kinds of stuff. I'd just do things just to be doing them. There was a lot of stuff that I did that was just outlandish and things were getting stupid. Finally, in late January it came to a sliding, screeching halt. Mother said, "That's it, you're gone, no more, it's over." And that was it.

She didn't actually kick me out. It was to a point where she would see me and curse. I mean she was tired of me. I could look at her and tell she would like nothing more than to deck me if I even looked at her. It was so hostile I said, "Look, Mom, why don't I just pack up and leave 'cause you're going to kill me or something." It was really that bad. So that's when I tried to leave. It was like one time she kicked me out I was gone for two weeks. That was the longest I had been gone previously. I came back and tried it out for a day. I tried it and it did not work and that's when I left and I haven't been back since.

Her body language was saying it. The last time I left, she didn't say to me, "I want you out of my goddamn house," like she usually says. When I left for a two-week period she dropped me out of school; that pissed me off because it put a hole in my plans. She dropped me out of school illegally. She thought she had me out of school, I thought she had me out of school, I was upset. I bought it out. That really made me crazy because I had planned to either repeat the year or go to some other school or take my test at the end of the year and get some credits. As much as I do stupid things, school was always a priority, as weird as it sounds. I had every intention of going to school. I just wasn't doing it the way she wanted me to. I had no intentions of being a drop-out or flunking out. So when she dropped me out of school, I went off. I just bugged, I was gone, that totally upset me, just made me crazy. So I went through hell and high water and I got back in school. I had the principal on my side, the vice principal, guidance counselors and social workers that loved me, so I did a little bit of this and a little bit of that. I had a whole army behind me. So I got back in school.

That made mother very upset. Now this is power struggle time, so Mother exercised her power and I exercised mine and I won. So she said, "You are not staying here, you can't outdo me, no; go." She didn't even want to talk to me, she was so pissed, so she wrote down that I wasn't to go to school anymore. I wasn't to see Damien anymore. Now little things I didn't mind, like, Damien, because I was ready to write him off anyway. I had to get a full-time job, I had to pay her seventy-five dollars a week rent. She had a whole list of stuff, some of it was cool and then again some of it was, like, uh huh. I read it, I didn't like it, I threw it away, and I packed my stuff and that was the last I seen of my mother.

Somebody gave me the number to this runaway program and I called. I went in and out of the place for a little while and then another program; I bounced in and out of there too. From the time I grew up, Mother would like say to them, I want him home, and when I say can I come home it's like no. So she was like playing this game, so one day she played it and they sent me home; I got home and she was ready to kill me. I mean we was fighting, she was throwing shit at me, she was like I don't want you. She bugged out in the morning so I slept there in fear, thinking, god, don't shoot me please. I was really on petro that night, cause I had never seen her so mad. As mad as I've made her sometimes I had never seen her that mad in my life.

She was in the middle of reprimanding me about being a bum and not having a job and I got called for a job interview. The phone rang and it was for a job and she's cursing me out. She goes to the phone and comes back and says get on the phone for a job interview. I thought that was kind of funny.

I went to counseling for a long time. I saw Dr. Morrison for a while and I saw Miss Tolpher for a while. I was ready for it, you know, but when it came down to me and Mom, I knew my mother wouldn't cooperate. I told Miss Tolpher, "Don't bother, you're wasting your breath, don't call." But she would get on the phone anyway and try and do it. Mother's not going for it, she will not go to counseling. As far as she is concerned there is nothing wrong with her, she's fine. This one brave woman was a little insane. She took me back to my house and sat with me with my mother and tried to talk to us. I was cursing her out, don't do this, she is going to kill you, you're crazy. She took me home and we sat there and we talked; it didn't work.

I'm not going to lie and say I never wanted to go home. I always wanted to go home, but I know my mother. I know that she had made up her mind this time that I am not coming back. Period. As much as I wanted to go home, I realized it was not a possibility. After that's when I started falling into the hard times, that was my nice four months up there in the cold. I was out there for like about a week, a week and a half. This was on the street, I mean—well, actually, I lived pretty well, I had friends, you know, so I was living pretty well. I'd crash one night here and one night there, that kind of thing. You know, I'd spend the whole day in school and then at night I'd crash at my friend's place. I began to crash here and there and everywhere. That lasted about two weeks and then after that, it wasn't that they said we don't want you anymore. I decided, I love you guys, so I can't do this to you. I got to find something of my own. So, I hit upon hard times for a couple of days, sacked up in the stairwell for a little while; it was cold, but I managed.

I used to live off a dollar a day. I could always get a dollar from somebody. I wasn't eating, so when I got a dollar I'd eat junk food. My meals came few and far between, so when they came I ate. So after about three days of the hard living, getting cold, I'm like ahhh. So that's when I said okay, fine, call the woman, so that's when I called, the other runaway program. It was great, but I still had a little problem—I was not going to school, period. That was the bottom line, I was not going to go to school; I already had my plan there and my plan did not include going to school. But at this runaway shelter, if you're going to be there you're going to school. Or you have to work full-time, but I don't work. So, I didn't want to work and I didn't want to go to school.

I worked at McDonald's once for a month. I was at home at the time. That was cool but something happened, Mother got in the way, the job blew up. I stayed at this shelter for two weeks, and I got discharged. I got discharged to go home and again that did not work out because Mother went and played her little games so, it's back on the street. I don't think I even went to the crib, I think I just went straight back on the street again. So, this is the middle of February and I was just running around trying to find somewhere to go. I'd break into the school, sleep in the school sometimes, I'd sleep in the stairwell in there. Once in a blue moon I'd crash at a friend's house, but this was very rare and then I came across a friend of the family's. He's got a little family, you know. I've been friends with him for a very long time so you know that was one of my long crashes. I crashed with him for about a week, but again it was the conflict of interest. He said if you're going to stay here you're going to work or go to school. I wasn't doing either, so I had to go from there.

What I was doing was going to the studio, writing rons, hanging with my boys. I lived a pretty normal life until it was time to go to bed. I'd go to school, you know, hang out, go after school, hang out, and then of course there was the meetings with Ms. James. I also got into a little problem because there are rivals here and they like to mess with you. So during my speak-out time I said something. Well, one of my friends got jumped by a posse of guys just for the heck of it and I didn't like that. They jumped him and beat him up for no reason. It was something to do. I didn't like that so I went and got a couple of my friends and we went over there and tried to take on about thirty people. Well, we all did it! Anyway, I wound up getting beat pretty bad, actually not that time. What happened was we won that fight, we took on a nice posse and we beat them all down and we left. However, they got revenge. They caught me a bit later on, like this was early March, they caught me and beat me down. So much for that idea, so that was the last time I raised any cane with a gang. Again Ms. Tolpher was there to help me and take me to the hospital.

During that time there was something strange going on because I had found a friend to stay with. This was a really good thing 'cause it was a friend of my mother's but the kind of friends you call once in a blue moon but they are good friends of yours anyway. She lived right around the corner from my mother, but I was staying there for a while and it was cool. Her son was going to a private school and I was going to the high school and I was staying there for a good two weeks. I was getting ready to get a job and things were working decent, but then I got jumped, and then there was a problem because Mother had to be called. So my mother and my friend's mother got into a conversation and then it was time for me to leave there. Once again I feel Mother's rap wherever I go. I just feel it and Mother gets me. So, after that I had to get back on my feet again and try to find something else. During that time things were the worst they ever got. I think what really kept me going was like my friends. The friends of mine that knew what was going on, I felt obligated to them because they were watching me and they were, like, is he going to make it, is he going to get through this, I mean is he going to give up and die and let the world walk on him or is he just going to make it through this? I always used to preach to them, if you believe in something you can do it. I didn't believe that myself but I used to preach that, I felt that all eyes are on me. Now, am I going to let this thing beat me or am I going to come through this? So, I think when it was getting really bad, I used to think all right, supposing I do give up and it all ends, so what? They are all going to look at me and say, ah, he didn't make it, and move on. I felt like if anything I'm doing it for them because there are people counting on me to come through this. People were like coming to me saying,

"Chuck, I don't know how you do it, man, you got no home, no money, no job, and you're looking decent." I was amazed at myself sometimes.

I was doing all right and I would work off and on. My rapping career was holding because I was doing too much stuff. I was basically just trying to live. I wasn't getting involved with anything but then another thing came along with this girl. She wouldn't let me go, she wouldn't let me do myself in. Every time I was ready to end it all I knew all I had to do was call her and she'd scream at me, yell at me, and get me back going again. And she kept me going. Samantha was doing her job too, as quiet as she was, every now and then she would come out of her shell and say don't you dare die on us.

I wanted to go home. As much as I knew it was impossible, in the beginning, I hoped she'd come around. People would coax me and say come on call her; I tried but I said when it became evident to me that it was not going to work I said fuck it. I just didn't bother anymore. So things are getting bad now and this is early April. Finally, like, I said, that's it, I've had it, I've got to do something, so I decided to go to DSS and try and get some public assistance, do something with myself.

For some reason Mom had always been right. Everything she said about me happened. She said, "One day you are going to cross me and it's going to be over." Sure enough it was over, everything she said was going to happen was happening. If you say I'm going to be a bum, I'm going to be a bum. I had no choice. There was no way I was gonna go down the tubes without at least somebody trying to pull me out of there, man. At the DSS I said, "Help me please," and I'm getting the bureaucratic runaround. And then low and behold, who comes and saves me, a knight in shining armor with an Afro named Len Thompson.

He happened to be walking through the hall and he heard them, they were getting ready to send me somewhere that I shouldn't have been sent just to get rid of me for the day. Thompson overheard what they were doing and said, "I've got to take him." I'm sitting in the room and I have hypoglycemia and if I don't eat before a certain time I get very weak. I had had an attack, I was lying there like half knocked out, and Len Thompson walks in and asks, "Are you all right?" I had never seen him in my life. I said yeah; he said, "Let's go." I'm like—what? He said, "I'm your father." I sat there and said, "What"? And the lady was shocked too. He said, "This is my son." At the time, I was hungry and I wasn't thinking. I was tired. If you're my father let's go, fine. So I got up and we left and he took me to the place where I presently reside which is called the Greenhouse. He's the director. That whole train of events was like a twilight zone.

The place was like a long-term group home. It's for cases like mine; you gotta be gone for a while. Very honestly the place sucks, but there is a roof over my head and it's food in the belly. I can stay as long as it takes. That's why I was very happy to be here. You're supposed to go to school, you're supposed to do this and that, but they don't enforce their rules.

I had found a place to live okay, a round of applause, but there were still problems. I found out Mother was playing a game with me the whole time. She knew everything that was going on the whole time I was on the street. I never knew that. I found out through Mr. Thompson that my mother knew about the whole thing. I was upset. Mother was calling the school, she was calling my social worker, she was calling everybody. There I am thinking that Mother has written me off to die. Meanwhile I found out Mother just had her little book of everything I did. She knew everything I had done.

When I first got to the Greenhouse it was rotten because Mr. Thompson wanted to get me back home. He wasn't aware of what was going on and said our goal is to send you home and I said don't waste your time. He says it's a piece of cake, I can get you home, and it's been eight months! We had a conference like a month ago and, you know, I'm a nosy little sucker. I read everything, found my case, and under contact with parent it says called regularly. Mother is just checking me out all the time and here I am thinking it's all over. We had a very, very strange relationship and as much as we would go at it and fight, there is nothing that she would like more than to have me around and there is nothing I'd like rather than be home but, we just simply can't.

I got into some major trouble and the Greenhouse was a madhouse. The kids there were too much. There were seven of us. When I got there, there were these two, one guy, a great big ugly sucker, he kind of ran the house. He was a resident. I didn't have problems with staff until recently. I was very radical so I walked in there with my mismatched sneakers on and my loud shirts and everything else. I had my own room and most of them there were two to a room. They didn't like me 'cause I was kind of uppity. They were all just insane so, I gave them a chance for about a week. I discovered they were all animals. So that's when I decided, I'm out of here, so I didn't spend too much time at the house. I pretty much slept there and ate there and that was it. I got back on track with rapping again and going to the studio. I got things back on track and I started preparing for either summer school or doing a year over or whatever I needed to get ready for.

The thing with Tina pretty much just fizzled, but then this thing with Samantha started escalating. She came out of her shell totally and we started talking about things and we started getting a little bit close. In early June something happened. We had been talking. I'm a very intense person when it comes to women so I was discussing marriage. It might seem outlandish but we are old enough and it was a possibility. So we were getting like that close. So one time, in early June, we went to like the lighting booth; we had an argument. We had this major argument, she was leaving. In the back of the school there is this hill you can walk up to the back and then you can leave out the front gate. So she's onward up this hill and I'm watching her. I can't believe I said that and I got mad. I got very mad and so I ran downstairs and out the door, and ran up behind her. I jumped on her and knocked her down and I got on top of her and I started swinging at her and I was like gonna do something but I said wait a minute. You like this kid. You can't do that. So I controlled myself and I stopped and she's crying her eyeballs out and I'm like trying to comfort her. I managed to calm her down; we went inside the theater and went into the light room. It's a very secluded place. In the lighting room no one would ever know you were in there, no one can hear anything. You don't even know where it is if you don't know the theater. So, we went in there and we were talking and whatnot and then, you know, we calmed down and one thing led to another and we were messing around and xxxxxxxx and then she had to go. By this time my adrenaline is pumping and again, I broke and I attacked her and we got into this major physical fight in which I broke her nose and some charges were brought up against me. I escaped with an ankle injury and she pressed charges against me and I went to jail. Usually if I'm going to lose control I go somewhere, I'll hurt myself, I'll curse out a wall. I don't like to hurt people. I was very upset that I hurt somebody that I cared about especially; I couldn't believe I did that. So, I went to the psychiatric ward. I was bugging out, I was absolutely going crazy. I cried for like three days straight, I wouldn't stop crying because I was very, very upset that I lost control.

I was in the psych ward for about a week and when I got out of the psych ward I turned myself in. Here's where the traffic ticket got me. I turned myself in. What should have happened was, I turn myself in, I get an appearance ticket, and I go to court. They checked me out to see if I had any outstanding warrants. Guess who didn't pay my traffic ticket: Mother!! So, twenty-five-dollar fine. I had empty pockets, I go to jail. Once in jail I spent the night in the pokey and the next morning I went to court. There were all these problems; they sent me to the county jail for ten days.

That would be a book in itself. Jail was too much. You talk about a scared brother. I mean, I used to steal, I used to shoplift, I used to embezzle, I used to do all kinds of crimes but I never got caught. I said that's one thing I'll never do is go to jail. I was confident. I went through being a runaway, I was on the street, and I still didn't go to jail. Low and behold, I go turn myself in and I'm sitting in jail. Again I was sitting there thinking Mother was right. Mother was always telling me, "You're going to go to jail," and I was, like, no I'm not, I'm not going to jail. Here I was sitting in the county jail surrounded by thieves, murderers, rapists, and I'm like I don't believe this. So, I went to jail for ten days. That was great, that was an experience in itself.

The day I got out of jail, the following day I was supposed to go to summer school, no problem. I went to summer school. I passed with flying colors and I only needed two credits more to pass high school. So I devised a plan where I would try and get an independent study and then get my last two credits and then maybe go on to college. Now, during this time I had a conditional release. I had to stay in the program and I had to finish summer school and appear at my court date. That's when they would decide my fate. So, being the wise person that I am, I figured, now, I have three months to convince the court that I didn't have to go back to jail. Samantha didn't press the charges. Samantha and her family knew that I would never, never, ever do something like that unless something was bugging me.

They had a protection order against me so I couldn't get near Samantha. I was screwed but I had friends who were close with her and they would communicate with her. I knew that her hands were tied because her parents were trying to do me in. The charge was rape, by the way, so I was under some heavy charges, so like I had three months to do something fabulous. So, I completed summer school and then I got involved with this group that was very, very antidrugs.

Amazingly enough, I was never into drugs. I experimented, you know, but that was it. I don't drink, I don't smoke. This is all the amazing things, you know, I'm just a regular dude who came upon some bugged-out parents! I'm not your average cliché runaway. This guy who has been abused, on drugs, no, I'm just the average run-of-the-mill dude. I did some things like, I didn't go to school but that's the only thing and all this stuff happened. But anyway I got involved with this lady named Linda Morton. She's twenty-two years old. She's a very good friend of mine and I had never known her until now. We have gotten to be real good friends.

Getting back on the street after jail was not nice. They released me back to the Greenhouse. They put me back and I'd stay in the program but, you know, back on the street, rumor was out that I had raped a girl so being back on the streets wasn't all that great anyway. I was conditionally released. They didn't pay my bail but on my next court visit a friend of mine, actually, a case worker at the House, Mr. Block, vouched for me. He promised that I would do this, that, and the other thing so I was released from jail. So I completed summer school with flying colors and then I was getting together with some of my friends and we wanted to do something major. So, I said, well, I'll do an antidrug rally. It'd be cool—

it'd be major and I didn't want to do it but I'm thinking I've got to impress these judges. So I'm going to do something heavy to make them see I'm a big guy. I behaved myself in the project like I always did, but, you know, I was never a bad kid. I'd pass school with good grades and I did this antidrug rally and it came off pretty well and got involved with Miss Morton. I was learning some politics, you know, we got some news published from channel twelve, got in the paper. I was just running around trying to get my life in order. So, I did the antidrug rally and that came off pretty well and from there we started an organization called SSO: Secret Society Organization.

There was a singing group called Secret Society in my rapping and we merged to form this group that's antidrug. We start tutoring programs in elementary schools, we take variety shows to the schools, we do talent shows . . . it's gotten pretty major, within like two months. It's all run by kids, high school students. My school gets a very bad rap for a lot of things—crime, low school grades—so we are trying to show that the kids can do something nice. We ain't so bad after all, you know. And we have been doing a lot of good stuff with the SSO and after the drug rally we were planning some other things.

Then my court date came up. So, this is the day of reckoning and I'm scared to death. I had a nice fat file. I had newspaper articles and TV coverage, man, nothing but good reports, so I walked. And that was like ahhhhhhh . . . And so since then life has been quite normal.

All this changed me. I did an about-face, like I was facing north, now I'm facing south and I'm running south. I was always very, very conservative, I was very shy, very introverted. I didn't have a lot of friends, I didn't go anywhere. There was a lot of stuff that I didn't do, being through what I've been through. I was kind of forced to turn around and just take on everything. 'Cause I was dumped on. It was like okay, kid, you want to go out in the world—my mother was like okay, and popped me in the world. Wow, it's a big place out there, so I was kind of forced to learn how to play the games and systems and things and survive. I'm just surprised I made it. And you know, now my life is pretty much normal. I got out of high school two weeks ago and finished my assignments. So I'm a high school graduate. Some people look at me and wonder, how did you do that? I got a job as a dispatcher for a tow company and, you know, I'm getting ready to go to college and people look at me like, how did you do that?

I want to go to college and study communications. I want to talk to somebody and let them know what's up. I want to get into writing, acting, that kind of stuff. I think there was a part of me that wanted to go through all this because a lot of doors opened while I was on the street and I could have easily, easily—I could have spent less time out there than I did. But I had gotten to a point where I was very, very antirules. I just don't believe in rules. When there are rules set to me I would rather walk around them, walk over them, go through them. I don't follow rules. If you like suggest something I'll consider it, but this whole thing with rules, that kind of thing is probably my biggest problem.

Contact with my sister is very loose. When I got to my cousins that was my closest contact to her, I found out she ran away, she got pregnant, and then she had the kid. The kid is in foster care with the first kid. She's had two more since then. Okay, she got married. I have bits and pieces of information about her. I haven't had contact with her for about two or three years. Then she was still local so I could find her and now she's gone. But my stepbrother is a private investigator so we are going to try and find her. I walk in to the Greenhouse one day and he's there, and I don't believe what I'm seeing. After that we were always close 'cause he was the one who was contacted about me. All of my brothers and sisters are in their twenties and all out of college doing their thing. But we are all pretty cool together. Me and my stepbrother feel that we have gone through a lot. I'm trying to do what I can to make things a little easier.

In the future I see myself as being very rich! Because, I'm either going to make a record or make a movie or something. I'm going to do something major soon. I do too much not to do something where I can make some money somehow. In the meantime I'll be here at the Greenhouse until I want to get out there on my own. I'll do the wild thing but that's after I get settled, and of course there is always—I want to go home. It's never going to leave me, as much as I have been through, as much as I know it's not possible—it's just natural, you know. I'm the baby and I want to be with Mom. But now it's been so long I've gotten used to it. It's not as big a bite to chew as it was before when I felt I'm never going home. Now it's like, okay, and move on. I don't spend a lot of time trying to analyze not going home. I'm very cynical these days, my personality has changed so much. I'm very cynical and very, very, very set, very sarcastic about things. There are a lot of things about me that have changed. I'm very liberal, laid back, I have pretty much a "to heck with it attitude" about things.

I always had somebody to tell me, you can make it, or I always had some way of expressing that I wanted to make it. There are cases much worse than mine. If I met a kid in a similar situation to my own I would just say, believe in yourself, depending on the intensity of the kid. That's the one thing I never did. I never believed enough in myself. I had people believing in me so I made it but if the kid believes in himself in his heart that he or she can deal with the situation . . . Set your goal and say I'm going to get out of this, okay, I'm going to make it through this. This is bad but there can be worse. I'm alive, I'm in good shape, I can get out of this. If you set your goal and believe in yourself and believe that you can make it through even the worst—then you can. Look at me now, I'm all right, you know, I could have been in some pretty bad shape, but I'm here. X mom, x dad, x that. *I* want to get out of this—*I* want to make it. You build from that, everything else falls into place.

I think my kind of story is one you need to hear. I'm like one of your cliché success stories. When it was happening I felt, it's never going to happen, I'm not going to make it. But you know, I did. Now I can just look back and say, hey, as bad as it gets it's not that bad as long as you believe in yourself. You just deal with it and get through it, and thinking back I don't have any problems talking about it. I used to, but now it's like, hey, it happened, it's in the past, now move ahead.

Elizabeth
(nineteen years old)

I was born in 1969 in a small city. I was told that my mom was still in high school; she met my dad through his sister and they started seeing each other. My grandparents really didn't like it. My mother ended up pregnant when she was eighteen. She graduated from high school and I was born in November. They got married in January. It was one of those things where girls don't do that and they got married because they were having a child. And, that's all I basically know, just that my mom got pregnant when she was very young and my dad was only nineteen. They got married and moved away.

For a while—I was probably a year old—we lived around my relatives, where I live now. Then we moved from there to someplace else, I don't even remember. I believe we moved because my father's family was up there, up in the northern country. And, I remember when I turned four, two of my brothers had been born and we moved back to the area where we live now.

I remember when my parents set up their trailer on my grandfather's land. I remember running around and playing, I remember what it looked like. And I lived there ever since, except for the times when I was in the runaway program and when I lived with my grandparents, but they live right down the road.

I spent a lot of time with my aunts, my mother's sisters. They were like my big sisters because they weren't much older than I was. So, they used to baby-sit me a lot. I am the oldest grandchild so all the little kids were younger than I was. My aunts were older so of course I wanted to be with them. I spent a lot of time with my grandmother. I remember stories they told me about how I was very frightened of my father. He would say sit and I would fall and sit.

I am still afraid of him now. Because be drinks; he's very violent when he drinks. He frightens me. He's verbally abusive now as he was then and basically that is the reason. He really scares me. My brothers were very frightened of him as well. He would come home and be very loud and aggressive and very violent. He'd pick up things and throw them across the room and he would hit my mom. I remember many times I just would sit in the corner and cry because be would hit my mother or he'd argue with her. I think that's why I was so afraid of him.

I don't understand my father even today. I understand him a little bit more, but I still don't understand a lot of the things my father does or has done. I have a pretty good idea, but I don't want to assume anything. He is not the type of person to open up and tell somebody. He's very discreet about things.

I started school when I was four. I went into kindergarten and I was afraid. I just remember little things like standing in line to go to the bathroom and the little sweater I wore. I would sit in the classroom and the teacher would be teaching things and I would never listen to her. But every time she asked me a question I knew the answer. She would always send reports home, and my mom would tell me, "You have to listen in class." I would say, "Mom, I know everything." I remember her giving me a lecture about that. The next day when I went to school, the teacher was talking and I got up and I started playing with the dolls. She asked me questions and of course, I answered them right. That really bothered her. But, that's about it. I just remember little things like sitting at a little desk coloring, having cookies and milk, making Easter eggs for Easter, and making things for my mother.

I don't remember elementary school very much. I was sick a lot in fourth grade; I had the measles and then I got the chicken pox right after. I was out of school for a long time, but I did very well. There are some friends that I have now that were my friends since kindergarten. But, I don't remember much, except going to lunch, getting drinks, things like that.

My dad would come home intoxicated. He would go to the bars or where ever he went after work and come home later in the evening, around 9:00 P.M. He got out of work around 4:00 P.M., and he would be intoxicated. When he came home he'd fight with my mother. She would make him dinner and sometimes he'd eat it, other times he would just throw it across the room. He would be mad at nothing. He would just be mad. He would come home and start yelling and screaming and carrying on. My brothers and I used to run in our bedrooms and hide and we'd cry. But I was always the one, I would always be the aggressive one to say, "We have to go out and help Mom," but they would never go.

My brothers are all younger. Bill is one year younger, Robert is two years younger, and my baby brother Seth is three years younger. So we're all right around the same age. They still have a difficult time, they sort of overlook a lot of things my dad does. They just ignore it, pretend that it's not there. They didn't feel the need to deal with it like I did.

I remember when I was very young we would go and pick my dad up from work. He worked at a dairy factory. I remember we were singing in the car and he'd bring us snack food home and we'd eat it, we were really young. And then I remember he worked for a company that paved driveways for a long time. Then he hurt his back and he's been out of work ever since. You know, I can't even remember when he hurt his back.

I was home when he was out of work. He was doing odd jobs on the side; well, he'd get a job and the doctor would say that he couldn't work so therefore he had to do other things. My mom would always do things to get by, like baby-sit neighbor kids or relatives. She always did things at our house, to make extra money.

If my dad couldn't see my mom, then obviously she was doing something wrong, like having an affair, doing something that he wouldn't like, like going behind his back and saying something about him. He was very paranoid; if he didn't know exactly what she was doing, when she was doing it, or what she was saying, he'd get very uneasy and he'd become verbally abusive. When he was intoxicated it would turn into the extreme, something that we wouldn't see when he was sober.

Mom cried a lot. She tried to leave so many times but she just never could do it. She would go to my grandparents, who lived next door, and my dad would always come down and get her. She would be very frightened and she would cry a lot. She was so afraid of him, not so much anymore, but before, she was petrified of him to the point where she didn't want to breathe unless he said it was okay.

I don't think she ever went to the hospital, but I remember times when she had black eyes and bruises and handprints on her throat for days. I remember a lot of the times when he would pick up something and throw it at her. He shot the TV out the window one time; he knocked over the couch when my brothers and I were on it. I remember one time I was only about four years old and I was eating dinner and he walked in the door and the next thing I knew I just hit the wall. He picked up my chair and he threw it at the wall. And I didn't even know what hit me, I just know I hit the wall and the chair hit me, I fell on the floor, and my mom was almost hysterical. She was crying at the time and all I did was cry. I didn't know why he did it, or what I did wrong. I was simply eating. So I went into my room and I hid under the bed. He was very abusive when I was younger. As I got older, he would verbally abuse me, as well as my brothers and my mom.

He doesn't hit anymore, basically because . . . I really don't know. I think part of it has to do with the fact that I ran away from home. I really have no clue as to why he doesn't hit her anymore. But he will attempt to and stop. She is still frightened of him in many ways.

It got harder and harder for me to deal with him. At first I told myself that I had to love him because he's my father and whatever he does is okay because he's my dad. As I grew up I began to realize that I didn't deserve to be treated like that. I realized that my friends were never abused. They always came from well-to-do families and their dads never drank to begin with, or at least their dads wouldn't drink to the point of intoxication. They would drink socially but not to the point of getting drunk just for the effect. I always wondered about that. I always had to question my mom and she'd say, "Don't talk about it. Just don't say anything or your dad will get mad." So I would shut up and leave it alone. But, after I got to be about fourteen I realized I couldn't deal with it anymore. I thought I was really going crazy. I wondered, why is he treating me like this? He doesn't love me and I'm his daughter. He beats my mom, he abuses me, and verbally abuses my brothers. It was a difficult thing to live with, so I just thought, nobody else is going to help me so I have to help myself.

I've realized that all through my childhood I was verbally abused. He would swear, he would come home and he would get me out of bed and make me sit on his lap and he would tell me stories about if I did this or that with boys I would end up pregnant or I would end up on the streets or I'd be raped. And he would tell me that I was bad because I had talked to boys. I wasn't allowed to talk to boys. He restricted me but he also told me that if I did certain things I would end up being a bad girl. I felt that I deserved to stay in the house because I thought my dad was doing me a favor by saying don't do these things and then you will have a good life. He started doing this when I was about twelve. He would constantly come home and make me sit on his lap and he would frighten me. He would always tell my mom to leave the room and then he would do things to me, like say if I ever did this he would kill me or he would threaten physical harm to me.

I could be fast asleep or I could be in my room laying on my bed just waiting for my dad to come home so I could hear the fights just to make sure my mom was okay before I went to sleep. He would come into my room and tell me to get up, or do things to get me out of bed so that I couldn't sleep. He would make me wash the walls in the bathroom or mop the floors. He'd just make me get up and sit on his lap and he would say really cruel things to me. He was very heartless in the way he spoke to me.

In some ways, I could never trust my dad and I was totally intimidated by him. Whenever he would come near me I would really become nervous and very frightened inside and I would start to cry. My dad has never sexually abused me—he would never dare, because my mom would really go off the deep end. But he frightened me because of the fact that he would say those things to me. Fathers don't say these things to their daughters. Most grown men don't say things like that to twelve-year-old children. I've seen a lot of movies on TV about how kids are sexually abused and things men say to them. My dad intimidated me and frightened me, and I couldn't trust him. I was to the point where I couldn't be in the same room with him alone.

I would tell my mother, "Don't you ever leave me alone with him," and she would always question, "Why?" I was just, like, "Mom, just trust me; don't leave me in the room with him." I would make my brothers stay with me; if my brothers were to go to their friend's house and my mom had to go to the store, I would make one of them stay home with me. I would tell my mom, "I am not staying here alone, I will leave." And many times my mother would go someplace, to the store for my father or something, and I would be stuck in the house by myself with my dad and I would just crawl out my bedroom window and go for a walk and he would ask me where I was, of course; I was doing something wrong because he didn't know where I was. I would go to my grandmother's and stay there.

My grandparents don't have a sense of what's going on even now. There are a lot of things they don't know. They knew that my dad abused my mom but they don't know about the things he said to me. My grandmother knew why I ran away, but my grandfather didn't even know why I ran away until right before I went to college. He never had any clue as to what happened. He never knew my dad beat me up, never. When he found out, my grandfather and I started becoming friends. Before he knew his attitude was, "You're a brat, you want to do what you want to do. You ran away from home just to hurt your mother," and he would just go on and on. He told me, "You'll never make anything of yourself, you'll end up just like your father." . . . and he just pushed all these things into my head.

I had a hard summer just living with my grandparents and trying to deal with my dad. I got into a really big argument with my grandfather and I was going to move out when my mom came down and she told my grandfather why I ran away and now he understands why I feel the way I do towards my dad. He understands now, so that helps out a lot. I just can't come out and say, listen grandpa, blah, blah, blah, and tell him my life story because my grandfather is very concerned about our well-being. He would be at my father's throat if he knew of any of these things. And I don't believe in violence so I don't want to harm my dad even though he may deserve to be hurt, even though he may deserve all those punishments, it won't solve anything.

It's funny, though, my dad would never strike me if I did something wrong; my mom would always punish me. She'd just spank us. After I got to be about twelve-years-old, I never got punished physically; I was sent to my room or I would have to sit on the couch for half an hour without watching any TV or anything, things to make me learn my lesson. But, I can't remember when it was that my dad stopped abusing me. He abused me as well as my brothers. When my brother was very young, I remember seeing him in the crib . . . he was crying. My dad hauled off and whacked him one and my brother was just, like—I don't know what happened to him, I think he knocked the wind out of him or something . . . my brother was so young, he was only about a year and a half old. He knocked him down in the crib and he knocked the wind out of him. He would spank my brothers with a belt, not for punishment, just to spank them, just in case they did something.

My dad would throw me across the room, he never used to spank me with a belt. He always hit me with his hands. Just his hands or throw things at me, in my general direction, just to frighten me. I can't remember when it stopped, I'd say around ten. He no longer hit me until I was fourteen . . . it stopped at ten and then when I was fourteen he beat me up.

He had come home and was very intoxicated. He was accusing my mother of being involved with the next-door neighbor. I had told him, "Dad, Mom was with me all day long, she was not out of my sight." All this man did was come up and bring corn—my mother had chickens at the time, and he brought some corn up for the chickens. Mom said thank you and he left. My father just looked at me, with this evil, evil look. He turned around and punched me in the face, knocked me on the couch, and I don't remember exactly what else happened. He beat me up, I had a split lip. He tore my shirt off, my clothes were ruined. He hit me all over. I also hit him back, which was the first time I had ever struck my father. He was also hitting my mother. When my father gets drunk he gets very violent and very strong. My dad has a heart condition, so that kept running through my mind, but I felt that he's hurting me and he deserves to be hurt back. I couldn't believe I was hitting my own father; even though he hit me, I still have to respect him because he's my father, I shouldn't be hitting him. But I did. I don't think the physical abuse hurt me as much as it did emotionally. Just the fact that my dad would punch me in the face, he couldn't love me. That's how I felt. I ran out of the house and went to the neighbor's house which was about five houses up the road. I stayed overnight there. Later on my mom came up to see how I was doing. My dad had taken off with the car and went out to look for me. My mom was torn apart. I didn't want to go home, I wouldn't talk to anybody, I just sat behind the couch and I cried. The next day my mother made me go home. I cried in my room for two days. My dad tried to come in and talk to me but I wouldn't talk to him. He touched my arm and I became very violent. I began hitting him and said, "Get out of my life." I was very upset and I told him that I hated him, that I didn't love him anymore and I couldn't believe that he hit me.

He was trying to apologize, but at the time I didn't want his apologies. I didn't want anything from him, just for him to leave me alone, and for about a month I wouldn't let him near me. I wouldn't talk to him. If he was in one room I made sure I stayed out of the room until he left. If I had to go to the bathroom and he was in his bedroom, I wouldn't even walk down the hall to go, I'd go to my grandmother's house. I always made sure that he was on one side of the house and I was on the other. Anything to stay away from him.

That happened during the summer when I was fourteen. I just couldn't deal with my dad. He would still come home drunk and he would swear and he would hit my mom. I wasn't doing well in school, I couldn't concentrate, I was very unstable emotionally. I would cry all the time. I couldn't trust anybody, I wouldn't let anybody near me. I just stayed in my room for a long period of time. I always told them, "I'm not going to stay here, I am going to get out of here, I am going to go away."

My mom had to go along with the things my dad said, just because he had some type of authority over her that I didn't understand. He would tell her something and she would automatically do it. If he said, "Jump," she would say, "How high?" and she would do it. I kept telling them that I was going to run away from home, that I was not going to stay there. I told them, "You guys don't understand, you won't listen to me." They wouldn't sit down and talk to me. All I wanted from them was their understanding, which they couldn't give because they didn't understand. They wouldn't even give me the opportunity to try to talk to them. I found out later that it wasn't my mom, it was my dad. So, when October came around I had had enough. The abuse continued a whole month and a half after the summer incident; the alcoholism, the fighting with my mom, the verbal and physical abuse of my mom all built up. He even threw the TV out the window. I remember once during that time he tried to choke my mom to death, and she was very sick for some time.

In my freshman year, I was on the volleyball team, and it was the first thing I had ever done. I couldn't continue in my sophomore year; my dad totally refused to let me play on the volleyball team or do any extracurricular activity. He didn't feel that I deserved to do it. He said that it took up too much of my time and I was never home. When I was home, he wasn't. It was only the time when I would start getting ready for bed that he would come home and do all this stuff. I didn't get a lot of sleep. I always made excuses. He always used to make me wear clothes that I didn't want to wear to school. He totally ran my life as well as my mother's. My brothers would just sit back and let it all go by because they were younger than I was and they didn't really understand what my mother was going through. They didn't understand a lot of things. My brothers basically didn't understand or maybe they didn't want to understand. Every time I wanted to talk to them they would cry. They would cry and they would get upset and they would say, "Don't talk about Dad like that."

My father never tried to control my brothers at all. They got to go outside and play with their friends and they could have friends over. I was never allowed to do that. The first time I had a friend over was when I was fourteen and it was the neighbor girl who they had known since the fourth grade. She was the first and only friend I ever had over. It was a one-time thing.

Sometimes if we would all go somewhere together, like fishing or hunting, my father would end up getting mad and turning around halfway there and say, "I can't take you anywhere." We would never go out to dinner, we would never do anything as a family, and we wouldn't even eat dinner together. My mom, my brothers, and I would eat at the table but my father would always either eat in the living room, or in the bedroom. He would never be a part of us. When he and my mother were getting along okay, he would take her out. One night they went out and they had dinner and my dad got drunk. I was watching my brothers at the time, I don't remember how old I was. When my dad came home I said, "Where's Mom?" and he said, "Oh, I left her there." "What?" I said. I was very upset and I was crying. Finally he went to bed. I tried to get my brothers to come with me to my grandmother's so that my grandmother could go to the restaurant and get my mom. I really think it was a bar. They were eating at the bar and something must have happened. So I finally went, and my brothers just stayed home and they cried because they didn't know what to do. They never had the nerve to go and do anything about it. When my mom finally did get home, my father beat her up and slapped me and made me go to bed.

He would not let me out of my room the entire next day. He called me all kinds of names and beat my mother up that night. Whenever I tried to ask my mom, "Why is he hitting you?" she would say, "Don't worry about it. It's none of your concern." Or, "It'll be okay, it's over with now." Or she would say things to me like, "Someday he'll get over this," or "He'll be punished." I have so many memories of little things that he's done. I understand now why I was so upset at the time.

I have always gotten along with a lot of people. I never really had any close friends, just because of the fact that I always felt that I was different, which, in fact, I was. They didn't understand a lot of the things I was going through. They couldn't understand. Because they didn't want to . . . and because of the fact they weren't in my situation. I had a lot of friends, but nobody I could trust. Until very recently, I still couldn't trust anybody except myself. I looked forward to going to school, just to be with people other than my family. My outlet was to get away. I did very well in school because of the fact that it was the best thing in my life.

I sort of lived two different lives. When I was at home, I was the hurting part of me. When I was at school, I ignored all the stuff that happened at home and just had fun and I was a kid. I was the person that I wanted to be. Like, the true person that I was . . . I was in school, and it was the only time I came out. When I was at home, I was a frightened little child that didn't want to do anything that Daddy didn't agree with or something that would make him upset so that I would be hurt. So, I just kind of looked forward to going to school to be with my friends and to just be a normal kid.

My dad was not a good person; he wouldn't even let me be with my grandmother. My parents would get in fights about whether or not I could go places with my grandmother. Mom would say, "Go," and I would get halfway out the door and my dad would pull me back and say, "No." I remember a couple of times when my father said that I could do something; of course, he promised me the world, and I had a world full of disappointments. So I never believed anything that he said.

He used to have this outlook on life that everything had to be bad or something always went wrong, to the point where you could never trust anybody and you are never supposed to be happy because when you are happy you are vulnerable. He would say things to me like, "You can't go to your friend's house because there are boys there, and if there are boys there you will end up pregnant," or "They're going to take advantage of you or somebody is going to rape you or you can't walk down the road even during the daytime . . . You can't walk from house to house because somebody is going to pick you up and take you away . . . and then they will beat you and rape you and kill you." Because he was my father, for a while I believed him. Then when I started thinking about all the things he was telling me, I didn't think anything could be that bad. Life is not that bad. People on TV don't have these problems, so why should I? Of course it is a fantasy world but I didn't know that at the time.

I never talked to anyone about what was going on at home. I never told anyone that my dad hit us. My friends would always tell me how they went rollerskating and out to dinner with their families and I wondered, why can't I do those things? What gives them the right to do those things and I am not allowed to? I felt like I didn't fit in with that group, although they were my friends and we had a lot in common. I just felt very uncomfortable and uneasy around them because they had so many more things to do in their life than I did. I would go to school, go home, do my homework, eat, and go to bed. We were able to watch TV—we were never limited to how much TV we could watch—but we were always in bed by nine o'clock. We would always eat dinner as soon as we got home from school and if dinner wasn't ready we would do our homework until it was done. We did our homework and then we would watch TV for two or three hours and then we went right to bed. It was monotonous. It was boring.

For fun my brothers and I would fight. We would literally beat each other up. We thought that was okay, when my brothers hit me I thought it was okay because my dad had hit me. I thought that was what boys were supposed to do to girls. I never hit them back until I got older and then I realized they shouldn't hit me. But that was about the only thing we were allowed to do. Just play with each other. Although I'm wearing a dress right now, I grew up as a tomboy.

Over the summer when I was fifteen, we had new neighbors who had a son about my age. I became very good friends with him, we were best friends, we were buddies. At the time I was a tomboy. We would play baseball, football, and all kinds of sports together. My father felt very frustrated with me and annoyed because I would spend so much time with this boy. His name was Mike and he came for the summer. He was here to be with his dad because his real mom lived in Japan with his stepdad. He came over to visit his real dad and his stepmom. We had a lot of things in common. He lived a few houses up the road so he would always come to my house and we would do things together. My father was annoyed with this. First of all, Mike was a boy and my dad had told me that I shouldn't have male friends. I spent a lot of time with him and my dad didn't like that. He was very angry with me because I spent all my time with a boy rather than a girl. He thought that Mike was taking his place and that I didn't need a father in my life anymore.

I had a terrible summer. Whenever I had free time, I would have to help my mother with the housework, and then I wanted to see Mike. I just wanted to be with him and have a good time. I could laugh and be myself with him. My father didn't like that at all. He would go up to Mike's house when he was drunk and he would say nasty things to him about me. He would say he didn't want him around his daughter anymore and if he ever came to the house again he would shoot him. He would just do things like that. My father would hurt me more than he would hurt Mike. If my dad loved me he would want me to be happy. He would tell me all these bad things that I was going to do with this boy and those talks started again. He would come home and I would have to sit on his lap and he would tell me that if I did this with Mike or if I kissed Mike that I would end up pregnant. He said I would be doing all these bad things behind his back and If I ever did end up pregnant he would never speak to me again and I would have to move out of my house. He always told me, "If anybody ever gets you pregnant I'll kill him." He frightened me and I believed him.

So I tried to stay away from Mike for a while. I was unhappy, which made me want to be with him more. And my father always thought that we were doing something bad, like we were having sex or whatever. That was a big part of the reason why I was fighting with him because he would not let me out of the house. He would not allow me out of my room unless he was there. This was in the summer and I wanted to be outside. If I went swimming I had to wear shorts that were almost down to my knees, a T-shirt, and sneakers. I was not allowed to go swimming without him being there. When he wasn't there I had to stay in my room, when he was there I could go outside. His bedroom window overlooks the field that we played in so he would always watch. He'd watch every move I made. And then he would report back to me. "I didn't like how you were playing this way and you bumped into Mike; why did you do that?" I would say, "It wasn't my fault." He would spy on me all the time. Once, I was allowed to go over to the next-door neighbor's house and play hide-and-go-seek, and he sent my brother out to check on me and see what I was doing. I ripped my pants because I was doing flips on their old swingset, so of course he thought that I was doing something bad. I wasn't allowed out of the house for a week. I was completely restricted to my room. And then at the end of the summer Mike went back to Japan and of course my dad was happy to get rid of him.

When I went back to school I started growing up and filling out, and that really irritated my father because I was getting older. I not only had one friend that was a boy, but I met a lot of boys. I would come home and talk about something that the girls and I did with a boyfriend and my father told me that if I was going to hang around boys in school that I couldn't go to school anymore. He wouldn't allow me to go to school. School was my only outlet, so I would always promise not to talk to the boys. So for a long time I wouldn't talk to boys, for like a whole month. Then at the beginning of October, I started to cry all the time. I wanted to be on the volleyball team but my dad wouldn't allow me to do that. I had to stay in the house and do something like wash the walls in the bathroom or mop the floor or dust all the corners. I had had enough. I decided to do something about it.

I tried to run away once before. I tried to go out my bedroom window with some of my clothes but my dad caught me. He threw something and broke my mirror. He was so mad and he frightened me. I don't think he was really trying to aim it at me but he smashed my mirror. I was really upset because he destroyed my property. I told him that I hated his guts and so I got grounded again. Then when they went to bed I snuck out my window and I started walking down the road and he came out and grabbed me. He brought me to the house and he threw me in my room and he told me if I ever did that again that I would really be sorry. I kept telling him all along that I was not going to stay there and that I was going away. I talked to a friend in school because I was really upset. I was late to class that day and I was crying. I knew that she was having problems with her parents and I asked her how she was doing because I was really upset because I couldn't deal with my parents. She told me that she was in a program, in a runaway program, and she was living in town. I asked her what kinds of things they did. She said, "They help you try to talk to your parents and understand them better," and she told me about a few of the things that had happened in the sessions with her parents. I asked her for the number. She didn't want to give it to me because she didn't want to be responsible for whatever I did, but I begged her and I got the number.

I called and I asked some questions. I talked with Donna on the phone, and I told Donna that I was having some problems at home that I couldn't deal with and I just needed somebody to talk to. I talked to her for about an hour on the phone. I told her how I felt and at the end of our conversation she told me, "Elizabeth, I think you know what you want pretty much and I think you have a pretty good understanding of yourself." She told me that the program was really busy and if I could wait a few days she would come to school and have a session with me. I told her yes at the time but I felt I really couldn't, and I believe this was on Wednesday.

I couldn't wait. It had gotten worse and worse every night. More things would happen and it would add fuel to the fire and I just couldn't deal with it. So I said okay, I could wait until the next week and have a session with her so that I could tell her more about myself and she could try and help me. I kept the number. On Thursday night I had a really tough time with my parents. My dad came home and beat up my mother. I just had everything I could take. I was hysterical and I was crying. I packed my clothes in a bag when I went to school on Friday. I ignored everybody and everything around me. I just let life pass me by for the day and I thought about what I was going to do.

I usually told my mom, "See you later." That morning I said, "Bye, Mom," and she just looked at me. I didn't come home from school. I went over to my friend's house and I was going to stay with her Friday night and call Donna on Saturday. I really needed to get out of the house because I knew that when my dad came home Friday night he would be totally plastered. I went with my friend. We were going to go to another friend's house and go to the movies. First we were going to go to the Arcade and then we were going to go to the movies. Just so I could get out and relax and do things. So we picked up our friend, and then went to the Arcade. A cop car pulled up so I went and I hid in the bathroom. I knew that they were there for me. I just had this gut feeling. My friend Erika came in and said, "Elizabeth, your dad is out here with the police and I can't lie to them. They need to know you are here." I fell apart. I was torn to pieces. I said, "Erika, if you were my friend you wouldn't do this." And then I cried for about five minutes and I realized I shouldn't expect that from her. I said to her, "It's really immature of me to want you to take responsibility for my actions. I am sorry."

I walked out. My father was getting cigarettes out of the vending machine. He just looked at me and he said, "You're going home." I said, "No, I'm sorry." I never really talked back to my dad before. I would scream and yell and cry but I never really looked at him and said "No, I'm not." I told him no and he said, "Yes, you are," and he grabbed my shirt and yanked it. The cop pushed us apart because I was ready to hit my dad. The first thing I thought of was to hit him to get him away from me. I wouldn't get into the cop car because he was going to make me go home and stay with my parents and there was no way that I was going home with my father. First of all my dad was drunk . . . he was totally intoxicated. He was staggering all over the place. I thought, here this cop is supposed to be the law and this man is walking around intoxicated . . . he comes to get you to find me and you're doing this. This is your job? I was thinking all this stuff and I wasn't listening to anything he said. My dad hit me and I said to the cop, "Are you going to let him hit me?" I was crying. The cop said, "I didn't see it." I said, "What? You didn't see it?" The cop said, "I think you are a brassy kid; you've got a lot of problems." I said, "*Me*? Dad's the one with the problem, he's the one that's drunk, he's the one that just hit me." My dad got in the back seat of the car and the cop opened my door and tried to push me in and I said, "I am not going." I was fighting with the cop, physically fighting with him and he was pushing me down. I would stand up and push him away because I was afraid that if I went home I wouldn't wake up in the morning. My father is really going to kill me, is what I thought. I was pushing the cop away and all my friends were standing in front of the building watching this. It was so humiliating for them to see my dad come in drunk and this cop taking me away. He pushed me in the car and locked my door. I was banging on the windows and my dad punched me in the side of the head. I don't know how he did it because he was in the back, but he hit the side of my head with this fist. Thud! This cop walked around in front of the car and looked in the window, he saw this. He told me that he didn't but I know that he did. I said, "He just hit me," and he said, "No, he didn't, I didn't see it." Then my father smacked me up the side of the head again and that time the cop saw it so he had to say something about it. He said, "Keep your hands to yourself." I said, "Is that all you are going to say to him?"

He took me to the police station and he locked me in a room because I was hysterical. I said, "I am not staying here and if you bring me back home you are going to have to tie me to the bed because in the morning I will be gone. I know my father is going to harm me in some way. He is going to hit me and he is going to beat me and he is probably going to kill me." I told him that he beat me up before and I know that if I went home he would do it again. The cop goes, "No, no, you're just a brassy young teenager, you don't know what you're talking about. You are just a brat," and I said, "You think I'm going through all this trouble for nothing." He just kept telling me to shut up and to be quiet. He said a few foul words to me that really ticked me off. I said, "I think you are stupid. I don't think you have any right to say those things to me," and I was going on and on. I was being very cruel to him. He locked me in the room and I banged on the door and I continued screaming.

He didn't make me go home with my father. He said we would drive around for a while. I knew that he was going to take me home, so I said, "No, I am not getting in the car with you." He let my father drive home—my father was totally intoxicated. He let him drive home! I couldn't believe it. Before he got me back in the car I was crying and I told him that I wanted to call this number. He said, "What is it?" I just called it the runaway program. He said, "You are lying, you are a liar, there is no such thing." I said, "Yes, there is." So he called the number and talked to Donna. I don't know what was said but we met Donna at a different police station. On the way he was trying to apologize but I wouldn't talk to him. I got to the police station and my dad and my mother were there. My mom just looked at me like I killed every feeling she had inside her body. She was very pale and she just looked at me like I was taking the only thing she had away from her. I looked at her and slid down the wall and started crying. Donna went in a room with my parents and they talked. My mom came out crying and Donna took me in the car. She took me someplace where I spent the night with a lady. In the morning she came to get me and we talked and we went to Darleen's.

On the way to Darleen's, Donna was telling me some things about her, but when I walked in I didn't expect her to be so young. She's only about twenty-eight or twenty-nine. She was very nice and told me to sit down. She got me a Coke and I played with the dogs. We took a little tour of the house. Then Donna left. Darleen gave me the biggest hug and made me feel so secure; she said, "Everything is going to be okay kid," and everything was okay.

When I came to the runaway program, people who didn't even know me cared about me. They were like, "Hi, you are a very nice person and we're concerned." They were there for me. When I went to my host family, I walked in and Darleen gave me a big hug. I thought, oh, my, there are actually people in this world like this? Living in an environment like Tim and Darleen's (my host family) was totally different than mine.

The understanding that I got from both the runaway program and them was a shock. I could talk with them and they would try to understand to the best of their ability. They would be there for me if I was upset. If I wanted to do something fun, Darleen and I would go do something fun. They were like a family to me. They were the family that I never had, something that all of my friends had and that I could never have.

I had a hard time adjusting to Tim because I had never sat down and talked to a man before. My dad would scream at me and yell at me and hit me but I could never talk to him. I learned a lot of things about myself and I grew up a lot while I was in the host home. People were there for me in a way I didn't know how to deal with. It was so overwhelming that it made me feel better about myself. The more I talked with Darleen and Tim, the more I knew I wanted to go to college. I didn't know to what extreme until I got there and they told me about how they had gone to college. I thought, Look at where these people are now. They have a beautiful home, they are well-off in society, and they have things that they want. They don't have any worries. Their attitude is relax and enjoy your life, it's what you make it.

I was there for about two and a half months. I had sessions with the staff and my parents, but my dad only came a few times. We tried to talk about some things we had problems with at home. I tried to explain to my dad, but of course he was very stubborn, and he wouldn't listen to me. That was a hard time in my life, dealing with my parents, trying to get them to understand me, sitting in the conferences with the staff and trying to get my dad to listen the few times he came. It was so frustrating . . . I felt like I was fighting a battle that I would never win.

I believe he was usually sober when he came for counseling. He had given up drinking after I ran away from home. I guess he changed a lot after I ran away from home. My mom said his attitude changed a tremendous amount and that he had stopped drinking. I thought everything was going to be okay. I wanted them to understand me before I went back into their house. I don't remember exactly what was said but we would talk about how my dad would never let me do things and how I felt. We would start arguing and fighting sometimes. He'd either make me cry, or I would just sit there and wouldn't talk to him. I didn't want him to be near me. The times that he didn't come I talked with my mom and she became very understanding and I understood her better.

My youngest brother's birthday present was to come and see me at one of these sessions. My grandmother came that day too. I got a new coat for my birthday. That was really good. You know, my dad came maybe three times. He came in and he would just sit there. He would be very passive, not talk, he let things fly by and he would ask, "Are you ready to come home yet?" I would say, "No, Dad, you don't understand.

All you are doing is just sitting there and you are not taking any of this in, you are not trying to deal with this at all, and I'm not ready." So he would get up and leave. And he wouldn't come back for like two or three sessions. Then he would come again and he would sit there passively and wouldn't really participate in much of what we said. He came again and he would say, "Are you ready to come home yet?" and I would say, "No, Dad, you don't understand. You need to understand me and I need to understand you." And that went on during the sessions.

I learned a lot of things about my parents that I never knew. I learned a lot about myself that I never understood before. It's not just what I learned out of the sessions, it's what I got out of the sessions. What I learned about myself out of the sessions, I sort of supplied to my dad. I had made excuses for his actions because he was an alcoholic and he didn't know how to care about people. I understood that I was a very caring person, that's why I was there because I wanted the home life that I deserved. I wanted my mom to be happy and be loved and I wanted them to love me and respect me as well as me respecting them. My dad had a hard life. He never learned to love anybody, he just didn't know how to deal with feelings. I tried to understand, I tried to make up excuses for him, to understand him better, a lot of the times it worked. A lot of the times it didn't. I was still frightened of him, I didn't trust him at all, I didn't believe anything that he said.

While I was at the host home, I went home for a day. I can't remember how I got home, I think they picked me up. We all went rollerskating . . . it was the first time my dad was ever on skates. We had a good day. We went to McDonald's for lunch. It was my dad and my mom and my brothers and I. It was the first time we had ever done anything as a family. I thought things were really picking up. My dad fell down, and of course I laughed; we had a good day. We had fun together, for once. They had asked me what I wanted to do the day I came home, and I said I would really like to go rollerskating. And they agreed. My dad said, "I have never been on skates before." I asked, "Well, could you try?" So we went and we had a really good day.

Then at the next session we just blew up at each other. We had had a good time and everything and then he said again, "Are you ready to come home?" Just because one day went well doesn't mean the rest of my life is going to be okay. I was, like, "No, Dad, I am not ready." I think that was the day that I just sat there and stared off into space. I wouldn't say anything.

Things at the host home were terrific. I got along well with Tim and Darleen. We did a lot of things together. Darleen taught me to cross-stitch and to sew. We did crafts, and I met some of their friends and their children. On Halloween I was just going to stay inside and Darleen said that I should dress up. I figured that I would stay inside and pass out the candy to all the kids. All the kids in the neighborhood came to the door, and so I was giving out candy and stuff and they invited me to go with them. I was pretty good friends with the two boys next door. Darleen brought me over to their house and introduced me to Roy and Mitchell and I became friends with them. Roy was my age—he was about fifteen— and Mitchell was about thirteen. So I went trick-or-treating with them, we had such a good time. I met a lot of new people, it was something that I had never experienced before. I had so much fun. In the past it was always just my mom and my brothers and I. We were only allowed to go in the neighborhood. Now here I was with people that I didn't know, I was very comfortable, and we became good friends. Darleen was really excited for me. She was, like, *go, go*. So I did go and I had a good time. They were very supportive of me in everything that I wanted to do. Darleen took my friend and I to the mall one time and we went skating together. Another time my friend's mom brought us to the mall and we went skating together. We went shopping at the mall a lot, things that I had never done before. I don't even believe that I ever saw a mall until I went with Darleen. I never even knew that such a place existed. We did a lot of fun things together, she was like a big sister to me. I could also talk to her and I could confide in her because she was very trustworthy; she would try to understand to the best of her ability. She gave me a lot of good advice about how to deal with things. After my sessions with my parents, sometimes I was very upset. I would go back to Darleen's and be very frustrated and I would tell Darleen. She would soothe my mind and told me that I would be okay.

Then my grandmother died, a few days before my fifteenth birthday. When she died, I felt very guilty. This was my dad's mom. I would call her up and see how she was doing three or four times a week. I had spent a lot of time with her when I was younger. She would come up and visit over the holidays and even though we only lived twenty minutes apart, my father would never bring me to see her. He just felt that I should be home even though he wasn't there.

When my dad was three he was eating breakfast and his dad had a heart attack and died. He had witnessed this and he loved my grandfather so much. He felt that his dad was taken away from him so he never learned to love anybody else or anything else because he felt that they would be taken away. So, he treated my grandmother as badly as he treated my mom and I. There were only certain times that he could talk with her and get along with her. All the other times he was very hateful, sarcastic, and mean. He loved her, obviously, and was torn apart when she died, but he would never say that. I would never hear "I love you" come from my father's mouth. And when it came to my grandmother he was very disrespectful. He would call her names. And, I wouldn't see very much of her after I turned thirteen just because he wouldn't let me. I wasn't allowed to stay overnight with her.

When my grandmother died Darleen was there for me as well as the program. I felt guilty because I was supposed to see my grandmother three days after the day she died. I was supposed to see her on Saturday and she had died on a Wednesday. I had run away and she didn't know why. She knew that my dad physically abused my mom, but she never knew what he had done to me. My grandmother was a very important person in my life. During one of the times I was having problems with my dad I would go and stay with her for a week or something and he made sure she called and made sure that I was not doing anything bad. When my grandmother died it was very hard because she was somebody who always understood the way I felt. If I told her I was happy she would be happy with me. If I was sad she would always try to understand why. I could never tell her about my father. I couldn't say, "Well, Grandma, Daddy does these bad things to me." I just could never do that to her. She was a beautiful lady and she was important to me. I felt like I had lost everything. I wasn't living at home and my grandmother had died. But, I had a lot of good things in my life. I had Darleen and Tim, the program, I was going to a new school, and I had different friends.

I left the host home right before Christmas. I was there about two and a half months. Leaving was very hard. I went home. I had seen my parents in the session and as usual my dad asked, "Are you ready to come home?" And it was one of those snap decisions that I made and I said, "Yeah." Just the fact that Christmas was coming up. That was the only reason why I went home. I didn't feel secure but I just did it because holidays were coming up and my mom always talked about me coming home for Christmas. So I said okay.

I was sort of excited. I went back to Darleen's house and I walked in and she looked at me. I just ran upstairs and I went in my room and I sat on the floor. I didn't know how to tell her. I didn't know how to say, "Darleen, I am leaving." So I just opened up my drawers; I thought, I have to pack because I am going home tomorrow. I went in to Darleen's room and I started crying and I said, "I'm going home tomorrow." She just looked at me and she was very sad and happy for me. She said, "Well, that's great, Liz," and we talked about the session and I told her that I had decided to go home. She said, "Okay, I am going to be here a bit longer so go and get your stuff packed." About a half hour later she came in and gave me a wall plaque that she had made with a little bear and a blue background. She was crying and she said that I am going to miss you and we cried for a long time and I finished packing. It was very hard to say goodbye to her. When I went home I cried. I believe my parents had a van at the time and when I got in the van I just started crying. My brothers were lugging my stuff into the house. I just started crying, and my mom asked me why and I just said, "I'm happy." That wasn't the reason; I didn't want to leave Darleen and all the security I had with them. I had the program to talk to, I had all these people around me, I was leaving all my opportunities to be myself, all the fun things I had were now gone.

I was going back into a house where I could never do anything before I left, why should I think that I am going to do anything now. So I went home and everything was so bogus. The first time I had gone home on a Saturday, well, it was fun and we had a good day. I took it in stride and kind of accepted it.

Then my grandmother died and I went home for the wake and the funeral and my father and I got into a big fight the day of the funeral. I was talking to my cousin and he said that I was sort of leading him on. It was my cousin, I mean, be real. So he called me a few names and I was very upset about that . . . he had not changed, he was accusing me of leading on my own cousin. I went back to Darleen's and I was very upset. I knew from that experience that things were not going to change this time. I knew that my father would never change. He would always be the same.

I pretended to get along and everything was going to be a little nice. Everybody is going to get along for a few weeks until I get used to being there. Then the real stuff will start and that's what happened. I knew deep down inside that's what was going to happen. Two weeks and things were fine. I could do anything I wanted anytime I wanted. We all sat at the table, everything was good. After I was home for a month, my dad picked up drinking again. I think he tried to go to AA meetings, but he couldn't because he didn't think he had a problem. So, he forgot that idea. He would always quit drinking for about three months. Somehow I knew that I would end up in that situation again. I was again in a very unstable home, my parents would fight, my dad was drinking. At least he had stopped beating my mom.

I couldn't deal with it because all I kept thinking was that he was going to hit me again. I still kept in contact with Darleen and my father felt very threatened by it because he felt she was going to take me away from him again. He took that out on me. He released all his bad feelings on me because he wanted me to be as unhappy as he was. And so I was in that situation again and I was very unhappy. I stayed with my parents until April when I moved into my other grandmother's house. She lived two houses away, but it was just enough space to not live with my dad but still be around.

When I moved into my grandparents' house in April I got a boyfriend. He was a kid down the street. His name was Keith. I spent all my time with him. Then he got hit by a car and I was at the hospital all the time. All my spare time was devoted to him. If I wasn't in school I was with him. At night I would be at my grandmother's house just long enough to eat and go to bed.

During this time my father and I were not speaking. We totally ignored each other; if I saw him I would go in the opposite direction. My dad was very threatened by Keith. I had no contact with my dad; we were not on speaking terms. I was spending a lot of time with Keith, and my dad was threatened by that because he thought Keith was taking me away from him. So my dad was making my life miserable. He would swear at me. He would call me names, he would tell my mother things that she would repeat to me: "Your father doesn't like you spending so much time with him," or "Your father doesn't want you at Keith's house when his parents aren't there." It just went on and on.

My mother was like a scapegoat. He would do everything through her. He would release all of his tension on her, he would scream at her, he would yell at her to get to me. And then I would do the same thing. I would go through my mother to get to my father. Being in the middle was not a good place for my mother to be but that's how it happened. When I lived with my grandparents, I went through a rough time, because my grandfather did not understand the way I was. My grandfather is a very hard person. He is not emotional, but he is a lot like my dad and he was also an alcoholic. He would make me get up in the middle of the night and get him a beer and fix him something to eat. He was just as obnoxious as my father, but he never harmed me in any way.

I did what I wanted, when I wanted. I also had no restrictions but I made my own restrictions. I took responsibility for all of my actions. I made my own curfew. I always made/sure that I was in by 9:30 on a school night; on weekends I was in by 12:00 or 1:00, even during the summer. Out of respect for my grandparents, you know, they were sixty years old.

The only thing I was involved in was Keith. I started seeing him and then he got hit by a car, so I was like pushed into this relationship without warning. I spent all my time with him. We developed a very good friendship and he was the only person that was in my life. He was the center of all my attention. That was really bad; I learned after two years that that was not a good place to put him. My father didn't talk to me because he didn't like him. Throughout this time I stayed with my grandparents. I would fight with my grandfather, because he didn't understand. He thought that I was being a brat and that I wanted to do what I wanted to do. I never told my grandparents a lot of the things that had happened just because I didn't want my grandfather to cause trouble. I didn't want anything said to my father because my father was having his own problems; he didn't need my grandfather getting on his case too. So I just let it go. I just let him say what he wanted to say to me. I fought with my grandfather a lot. I argued with him all the time. He would always tell me that I would never make anything of myself. He told me all the things my father told me. He didn't say anything about getting pregnant, but he would tell me that I would never amount to anything, that I would end up on the streets. Or he would say, "Get out of my life. I don't want to hear about you, just get out of my house." He thought that I was being an obnoxious brat. I had a rough time when I went there.

Keith was everything to me. I cared about him so much, I had nobody else I could talk to. Then Keith started treating me like my father treated me. He knew about what had gone on in my home and he had a lot of family troubles too. His mother was married five times. A long, long story. She would always interfere in whatever we wanted to do. If we wanted to do something she would interfere, she would be like my father. She did all the things my father did to me. She would swear at him and she wouldn't let him do things. She was very threatened by me, just like my father was threatened by Keith.

I really cared for Keith a lot until he started treating me like my father did. If I wanted to see him and be with him, he would say, "I am going to go do something with my friends, I don't care about you." So during this time, I really I had no idea of what trust was. I didn't trust anybody, not even Keith. I looked down on myself. I was so negative about myself and I was so unhappy. I wouldn't smile or anything. I would complain all the time, I would cry, I would just give up on everything that I started, I would not finish anything. Except in school. I did very well in school. I was on honor roll or merit roll all the time. I kept my work up, I just sat there, listened, and took tests. I never did a lot of homework, I just did what I had to do to get by, and I got good grades. So did Keith. His mom would always interfere and say things, like, "If you don't keep your grades up, forget about seeing each other," taking on the role of my father.

My father and I went through periods where we would talk for two weeks, we'd get in a fight, he'd come home drunk, and he'd start swearing at me. I would be talking to my mom and he would say, "Get out of my house, you don't belong here," and we wouldn't talk for six months at a time. He would sometimes try to do things, like for my sixteenth birthday he tried to make me a surprise birthday party, which was very nice. He gave me a party and lots of presents. What my dad didn't understand and what he still doesn't understand is that I am not a materialistic person. I care nothing about material things. He thought that if he bought me something that would make up for all the bad things that he did. But it didn't. I want understanding and that is all. I just want him to understand me. So they gave me a party. Everything was good, he was happy, and we talked for a couple of months. Then for the whole summer that I was sixteen we did not speak.

On my prom night my dad was not there. He went out drinking that day and he never came to see me. Keith and I went to the prom. Keith's parents were with us, so my parents approved. When he wasn't there for my prom night it really made me sad because I really wanted him to be there and see me. For the homecoming dance at school my brothers had to go with us so that they could keep an eye on us. My father would do other subtle little things in order to keep an eye on me. During the times that he wasn't talking to me he would go through my mother and my brothers. Then for my seventeenth birthday my mom gave me a party; my dad never came because he went out drinking. Right when the party was beginning to break up and I was ready to take my presents to my grandmother's house, he came in the door. He was drunk and he didn't say anything, he just walked by and went to bed. So I thought, "This is good, my father really loves me. Enough to come to my seventeenth birthday party! That incident made me feel very unhappy and unimportant.

We had Christmas, and I spent the night at my parents' house Christmas Eve. We had a terrible Christmas; my parents fought all day long. I went to bed hearing them screaming at each other in the bedroom and I woke up hearing them screaming at each other. It was a terrible day and I spent as much of my day with my grandparents as I could. At dinner my father got very upset, I don't know what his problem was. He ate dinner in his bedroom. My mom and my brothers and I sat around and ate Christmas dinner together. Easter came and was another one of those bad times. They fought and argued at the table the entire day. They were very sarcastic to each other.

My mom and my adviser at school were talking about college and I thought everything was a big joke. I thought, Well, I am going to college, and I didn't have to do anything to prepare for it. I thought the SAT was a joke. I did nothing. I didn't even know what the SATs were for. So when I learned all the things that I had to do to apply for aid and whatever, and that the SAT wasn't a joke, I was not happy. I was advised to take the SAT, so I took it. I did okay, but I took it a second time and I still didn't do great.

Keith was still in my life. But I was preparing for college and I was going through a very hard time with the relationship. That's when I started thinking. Keith's temper has just gotten totally out of hand. He was very jealous of my dad and he lied to me just like my dad did. He'd do all these things that reminded me of my dad. I would call him "Dad" and that would really get him upset and he would throw things. He had a very violent temper. He filled the role of my father and I expected him to treat me like that just because my father did. So I let it go, but after a while, I realized that I couldn't deal with this. I learned to dislike him as much as I dislike my father.

As a person, I don't like my dad. I mean I absolutely despise him. As a father, I love him mainly because it's expected out of me, because he is my dad. I see some good qualities in him. I mean he is human and he does have some good qualities, but as a person, I totally despise him, even today. A lot of things have changed, but I still have those feelings for him. They are not as strong as they were before but they are still there. When Keith filled the role of my dad and I began to dislike him, I just told him he had to change. I could really see my dad coming out in him in some ways and he frightened me. When we would argue I would just stay away from him because I thought he was going to hit me. But he never did. So around the beginning of the new year I told him that he either had to change or I was going to get out of his life because I didn't deserve to be treated like that. He didn't change and I broke up with him a week before graduation.

That's when all these changes started taking place. I had the best summer of my life. I moved back in with my parents; it wasn't so bad. My dad and I didn't really get along but we didn't fight. He knew that I was leaving within two months. So I had a good summer. I spent a lot of my time with my friends. My parents were still fighting, my mom was talking about a divorce. I just couldn't deal with it. But I did pretty much what I wanted to do. So I had a good summer, and then I went to college.

My dad always told me that I would never make anything of myself. I told my parents when I was in fourth grade that I was going to go to college and they never believed me. The day they took me to college, my dad said, "You know, you told me a long time ago that you were gonna go; I could just never see you going. I'm really proud of you." For my dad to say that to me, it was something. I felt like saying, "Thanks, Dad," and I walked in the door and cried.

The first week of college I was very homesick. I hated it there, the people were different than I was, they didn't understand me, they didn't know anything about me. And then I started to adapt and I began to like it more and more. By the end of October I really started feeling bad about myself. I got a boyfriend, and he's been in my position so he understands so much. His parents are divorced, his father was an alcoholic, his stepfather was an alcoholic, he went through all that stuff. He's very understanding and he's terrific.

His name is Jeff. My old boyfriend harassed me, that was the bad part, the link to my past. The feelings continued to haunt me. I would call my mom on the phone and my father would get on the other phone and he would be totally smashed. He would be drunk and he'd be talking and I'd say, "I gotta go." I tried not to think about it, but then I couldn't concentrate on my schoolwork and my grades were going down. I was carrying C's and I got in a fight with Jeff. It really started me thinking about, what am I doing to myself? I went and talked to a counselor about why I couldn't concentrate. All he did was listen. I told him how I felt and I said I couldn't concentrate, I couldn't study, I can't be in a room by myself. I feel very lonely and nobody understands me. I couldn't study, I couldn't be in a room where it was so quiet. Subconsciously I was think-ing about my mom at home. She was so unhappy and I was happy at school with what I was doing. I felt as though I was letting her down. I felt bad because she was not happy and I was . . . I felt that when I was unhappy I was giving them what they want. They just want me to be in their position. When I sat down to study I would get up and run around. I would try not to study. I couldn't be in a room by myself. I was thinking that the reason I was getting up was to subconsciously get away from those feelings and ideas and try to run away from them. Jeff and I argued because I was changing, and I was very preoccupied.

I was talking to a counselor and I just told him a little about my home life, how my dad was an alcoholic, and he gave me a book. It's called *Adult Children of Alcoholics* and the book is so me. I read the book and I was amazed . . . it felt like I was looking into the mirror and talking to myself. It all reflected back on me. There was a list of thirteen things that happen to adult children of alcoholics or things that they do. Ten of those things applied to me. I read them to my roommates because I was so moody. I wasn't getting along with them, I would snap at them and hurt their feelings. They agreed, "It is so you."

I had no self-confidence. I would always look to people for approval. I had a hard time dealing with intimate relationships like with Keith, because I felt all guys would be like my father. I just couldn't trust anybody. The only person I could trust was myself. When Jeff would promise me something I wouldn't believe what he told me. I started becoming jealous of other people around him. I couldn't believe what he was saying. He would follow through with his promises; if he said he would call or come by at five o'clock, he did. Usually people would tell me things and do the opposite. And for two days I just vegetated in my room and gave it a lot of thought. For once in my life, a promise was a promise.

I feel so much better about myself, after reading this book. I under-stand me better, I understand the reason I am doing these things. I am not distrusting people on purpose, it's just that my dad is coming out in me. His alcoholism is affecting me too. I was doing just what he did: I didn't trust anybody, I was loyal to people who didn't deserve it, I wouldn't believe anything anybody said, I was always looking for approval, I had no self-confidence, and it's easier for me to deal with negative emotions rather than positive. That is what I am used to and that is what he is used to and that's all he has shown me. I was hurting the people I cared about most . . . which is what he had done to me. I know my dad loves me, I know he cares about me, but he's hurt me and my mom and my brothers because we are the most important people in his life.

So the last week I was in school I totally turned around my personality and my perspective and I'm responsible for my own actions. I am more confident in myself, I know I can do it. I brought all of my grades up from C's to B's within two weeks because I just sat down and studied for my tests and I did what I had to do. I was able to concentrate.

I am totally relaxed and I trust Jeff now. We had a good week together; we talked. He is so understanding; he sat there and listened to me. I was upset about my grandmother dying and he understood because his grandmother just died a few months ago. We are on the same wavelength and are interested in the same things. I shared the *Adult Children of Alcoholics* book with him. He told me that he was proud of me. He said, "I can't believe you are doing this on your own. You overcame the first step which was realizing what you were doing to yourself and the second step you are dealing with." I said, "Yeah, and the third step is when I go home, I am telling my parents."

I've told my mom. I can't seem to tell my dad. So many things have happened to me recently. I've hurt people, I've hurt myself, and I am not going to do that anymore. I'm a good person, I deserve better things, I deserve the best out of life as well as other people do. Other people don't need to be hurt by me as well as I don't deserve to be hurt by other people. And I don't know. I am a lot happier. And I came home thinking everything would be hunky-dory and it's not but I am only here for a week and then I am back to school. I am just trying to grin and bear it; things will be okay.

I am taking special education and psychology. I am doing well; I was going through a rough time because I didn't understand a lot of the things I was doing and why. I got a lot of things straightened out so now I feel relieved. When I think about my home life, I think about all those bad things that happened to me and it interferes with all the good things I do now. So I am trying to deal with that and I have a lot of good friends who are very understanding, which helps. And they make me feel at home. So I am very comfortable socially, I am doing very well, academically—B's—I would prefer A's but . . .

I am working in the special ed building and I correct tests for professors, run errands, and do little things for them. I've decided that I want to go into special education. I love kids and I want to help them. I do have some disabled children in my family and I am very comfortable with them. I feel that that's what I want. I have this little theory about why I want to do it. It sounds strange but, I feel that other people should have the opportunity that I have had, to be the best person they can be and be proud of who they are by reaching their ultimate goal. Many people have helped me along the way. I feel that other people deserve my help, and since I am willing to give it, well, here I am.

Jozeph
(fifteen years old)

I was the only child my mother ever had. I've never had any contact with my father. My mother was an alcoholic and she couldn't handle me, so my grandparents took me when I was nine months old. I lived with them up until my thirteenth birthday. My grandmother is distant, my grandfather is an alcoholic. It's not something that we talk about but everybody knows it. It's something that people don't want to look at. My great-grandfather, he's quiet, he just sits around the house. He used to live in North Carolina and visit sometimes, but then he came to live with us permanently.

When I was still a baby my grandfather worked at two or three jobs at a time. He worked in a factory, he drove a delivery truck, he had a whole bunch of different jobs. My grandmother worked in a nursing home.

The first time I remember having contact with my mother I was about nine. I wasn't told anything about her. I always thought that my grandparents were my mother and father. One night I overheard them talking about the problems and how it was bad to bring in the third person. I didn't know then but I figured out later that they were talking about my mother. They thought that there were a lot of problems because my mother started coming back.

I went to a nursery school all day until my grandparents got off work. It was in a basement where all the little kids went. I don't really remember anything else. My grandfather wasn't home that much. He would go from his day job to his night job and then he went gambling from there when he got off.

My real mother was adopted, and so was my uncle. I don't know if that was because my grandparents couldn't have children or what, but they adopted them. I had an aunt who lived around the corner from us; she had kids. She was an alcoholic too, but my grandparents didn't want us to associate with her kids 'cause they were bad. There was an older one, one in the middle (who was around my age), and one younger. I also had an uncle and an aunt that lived across town. They had five kids but they are all a lot older than I am. They were in high school. The only time I saw them was at church or something like that. I didn't really spend too much time with anyone in the family except with my grandparents.

I was like the model child. I didn't do anything wrong because I didn't know anything else. I was basically sheltered. It was just go to school, go to church, and then back home. School was like a whole different world; that is where I met a lot more people, you know, when I was older, like ten or eleven. Up until then, church was basically my outside activity. If there was something going on at church, I went to church. Monday and Tuesday my grandparents had their choir rehearsal, and Wednesday night was prayer meeting, and Friday night my choir had their rehearsal, and Sunday was church. I was comfortable with it because I knew nothing else. I was accepted.

At nine I had my first contact with my mother. Before she came, there were letters and stuff sent. I found out that I had a different mother and that is when the visits started. The first thing I remember was she came down in a taxi because she didn't have a car at that time. She was recovering from the alcohol. She brought me some presents: a dictionary and a tambourine for church and some clothes. We spent some of the day at home and then we went to the mall and took pictures and stuff like that. At first it was just that one day and then it was about one weekend a month. It was fun, but I still didn't think of her as my mother. If I wanted something I didn't ask her, I asked my grandmother. I had thought of her as more of an older sister that was there to get me out of the house to go and do stuff together.

There were problems between my grandparents and my mother. My mother couldn't come down and stay the weekend because she didn't like the fact that my grandfather drank and she was recovering. My grandparents talked about how they didn't like the way she turned out. My mother said she just couldn't deal with that when she came down so she would stay for a day. Most of the time my mother and I would do something away from the house and then we would come back and eat dinner. She'd stay there for maybe an hour and then she would head back. When my grandparents wanted the visit to end, it ended.

The relationship between my mother and my grandparents wasn't the best because of how my mother was raised. It was sort of like a power struggle between my grandparents and my mother. They didn't really get along that well. When we were all together there was a fakeness to it because there were certain things we just weren't going to talk about. My mother had given the responsibility of me to my grandparents. My grandparents were holding on to that, and they weren't going to let me forget that and they weren't going to let her forget that either. My grandfather was drinking back then too. I didn't really start to notice until my mother started coming around. He would drink in the house but I never saw him drunk because usually when he got home from a bar I was in bed so I didn't see what was going on.

I got really rebellious. There was a whole bunch of stuff that I saw other kids doing that I couldn't do because my grandpa was very possessive and strict. I would get angry because there were little five- and four-year-olds that were staying out later than I was and their bedtime was later than mine. I was in elementary school and some of these kids hadn't even started school yet. I got mad at my grandparents for this from time to time. It was mostly with my grandmother because I was scared of my grandfather. After a while I started getting angry with my grandfather too and that was when things got bad with my grandfather. A year later was the first time I saw him drunk. He was coming after me and my grandmother stepped in between us and he sort of pushed her out. He didn't hit her, but he pushed her out of the way and I told him if he ever hurt her again I was going to kill him. After that I changed. Not because I wasn't scared of him anymore . . . it was because I was so angry that I just didn't really care what happened to me or what I did. So I started running away from home and staying out until four in the morning.

I first ran away from home when I got to junior high school. It was with a whole bunch of kids that I knew when I was back at the other school. One night we all just decided we were sick of it all. We just took off and there was this one part of town that we all liked to hang out in so we just went there. We were at my friend's house for a while and then we went over to the junior high school and then we just walked back home. It was three or four o'clock in the morning. Most of the time my grandparents were asleep when I got home, but I would have to knock on the door to wake them up because I didn't have a key. My grandfather would let me in.

My grandfather did the beating so I was scared of him. My grandmother would say, "I'm going to tell your grandfather when he gets home," so I would argue with her. Then she would just tell him about it when he got home. I can't say he beat me up—he never closed-fist hit me—but there is beating a child and then there is beating a child and he never beat me. They say you can whip a child or you can whop a child and whipping isn't as bad as whopping. My grandfather whopped me and mostly when he did that, he was strong. He never left black and blue marks but he left welts on the skin. When he hit me on my face and on my eye, it didn't leave a scar, but it felt like he knocked my eyeball out 'cause he has really, really thick hands. He either used his hands or his belt. He hit wherever he could get a hold of because when he beat me I tried to get away. At first I would just sit there and take it, but after a while I would try to get away. He had to chase me all around the house. Then he would pin me down and if my legs were what was there he'd do my legs, if it was my arms he'd do my arms. He never hit me in my back or in my face except with his hands. He usually sat on my chest when he did it.

When I was twelve I got caught stealing money from my grandparents. My grandmother gave me my grandfather's wallet to take back to the bedroom for him and I took five dollars out of his wallet to go to the movies. My friends were planning on going to the movies and they asked me if I wanted to go. I asked my grandparents and they said no. I wanted to go anyway because I had never been to a movie and I wanted to see what it was . . . so I took five dollars out of his wallet. I gave him the wallet and I didn't know he was going to look in his wallet or that it was the last five dollars he had. He looked in there and saw that it was gone and I tried to play it cool by saying that I didn't know what happened to it. He checked my pockets and found it. I got into trouble for that; he beat me and sent me to bed. My grandmother grounded me for a week and I couldn't watch TV or anything like that. I just had to come home, go to school, do my work, eat dinner, and go to bed.

Then I started getting into trouble in school. It wasn't that I wasn't going to school, but I was getting mouthy with my teachers. I was in the principal's office constantly and then I started getting into fights with other kids. I wasn't going out looking for fights, because I was quiet, but they picked on me. I still got sent to the office because we were fighting. My grandparents thought that I started it and that I was the trouble-maker, and so I would get beatings for that. And that was about the time that I decided I wasn't going to take it anymore and I just started leaving. I was running away from home but I always came back the next morning, like early in the morning, at 4:00 A.M. That went on for maybe a month or two and then I started staying away for longer periods of time. I found friends that would let me stay at their houses for a few days. How my grandparents never found out, I don't know because when I ran away, I was right across the street at a neighbor's house. The neighbors took a liking to me and they knew what was going on. So I would stay over there and I just wouldn't go outside. I'd stay inside and so they never knew where I went.

After that they brought my preacher home from my church because things really got uncontrollable. They were just talking, my grandmother and my grandfather and the preacher, going on about why is he so bad in school. I said, "I just want to do the things I see other kids doing, go out with my friends and have a good time." They asked me what I thought having a good time was. And I said, "Being able to do what a normal twelve-year-old can do . . . like going to friends' houses." They didn't like any of my friends. All my friends were unacceptable, and going to the movies or having birthday parties was out of the question. I had two birthday parties the whole time I was growing up, one when I was really small and one when I was like seven or eight. I would get invited to parties but I could never go because I had to go to church. My preacher said, "It seems like you got a lot of problems," and I said, "What if I do." Then he asked me what I thought I could do to solve these problems. He asked if these problems were about my mom, and whether these problems would be solved if I went to live with my mom. I said, "Yeah." I didn't take time to think about it . . . I didn't care, I just wanted to get out of there, so I said, "Yeah." He said, "Okay, fine, I'll send you to your mother's house."

My grandparents didn't really care what happened because they said they couldn't handle me anymore. My grandmother called my mother and said she wanted her to come take me. My mother moved out of the apartment she was sharing with someone. Since she had never lived on her own, she wanted to try it out before I came up there. She even got a better job. Then my grandmother called her up and said they changed their minds and decided to keep me. I didn't know what was going on. The preacher told me a little about what was happening, but my grandparents didn't say anything. I thought I was going home to my mother but then it didn't happen. The only thing I was thinking about was, anything would be better than this.

A few months later we had another meeting with my preacher. I told them that I didn't want to be with my grandparents, and everybody said okay, you can go live with your mom. Then she came and picked me up. I moved to another city with her on my thirteenth birthday.

That's what caused a lot of problems between me and my mother. I wasn't expecting her to act like a mother. I was expecting her to act like she did when she came down to meet me. When she took the responsibility of becoming a parent, I ran into a whole bunch of problems then too. We were going to wait six months and then my mother was going to see if she was going to adopt me. After six months all this stuff started going on with me and my mother too. So the adoption process never got off. I didn't even live there for a full year.

I got up there that Sunday and the next day she signed me up for school. I started school the very next day. It was late in the school year. I felt weird and the kids there didn't like me. My new school seemed to be behind the old school because when I started the work wasn't hard. I had done it in elementary school and this was supposed to be considered a junior high school. I got up there in seventh grade, and they didn't know whether they should pass me or fail me 'cause they didn't have my records. I went to summer school there and passed so I went another year at seventh and eighth grade. I made a couple of friends there. Most of the friends that I had there were rejected from everyone else so we had our own little group.

When I came to live with my mother I had all this freedom and I didn't know what to do with it. She had never been a parent so she didn't know how much was too much and how little was too little. My first night I had a twelve o'clock curfew, and this was a change from a seven o'clock curfew. I'd go out and stay up even though I didn't have any place to go. I didn't really do too much with my friends because we weren't that close yet, but I'd just go out and hang around anywhere.

At first I just hung around the house. Then I started coming into my sexuality. I started scoring in all these different places and I ended up in this park. I started staying there until eleven o'clock at night and then I would ride my bike back home. My mother got me started in a youth group at the community center. I met people from there too. One day I went to the movies and I was coming back downtown and I saw one of my friends from there. He said, "Hey, do you want to go to this juice bar?" I said, "Okay, sure," and we went there. It must have been close to 12:30 because the place didn't open up until eleven o'clock. From there I walked home. I didn't tell my mother where I had been or anything.

The juice bar is a nonalcoholic bar. There were people in there who were older, because I was only thirteen or fourteen and there were fifteen-year-olds in there. You were supposed to be eighteen and over because they showed porno movies. The next time I told my mother that I went there and she was okay about it. At first she didn't know what kind of place it was. I just said I went to a juice bar with my friend Craig. I went there a couple of times with her knowing that I was going there. Then a couple of her friends saw me there and she looked at the friends of hers that were going there and she figured out what kind of place it was. It's predominantly gay, but on the weekends everybody comes. It's where you go to after the real bars close. That's why they open up after eleven o'clock, because that's when they get the most business. From 1:00 A.M. until 3:00 it's packed; you can't walk in there. I didn't really have too much trouble with them asking me for proof of identification because they had seen me before. Then I started going there by myself and it started to be a drag . . . but the feeling of just going out and being with all these people felt good.

When I was thirteen, I met up with a whole bunch of people. Alex and Julie were boyfriend and girlfriend, but they were bisexual. I met Alex through Craig, the one who introduced me to the juice bar. I met Craig's brother, Lee, who was around my age. He brought me to the park and introduced me to Alex. We hit it off and became friends. Alex and Julie showed me the park and other places. I had been to the park a couple of times myself, but I had stopped going. They got me back into it. I started going there on a regular basis and I started staying out past my curfew. I was out more than my mother was. The park is a place where you go to have sex. I didn't go there for sex back then because I was too young to know anything about it, although I knew there was something weird about it. I wasn't like everyone else there, and so they introduced me to what was really out there. It was fun to do things I knew I wasn't supposed to do. My mother started saying stuff about what I was doing. She said she didn't want me to go to the juice bar anymore and I didn't like that. She didn't really know about the park then.

I guess that was the time I started running away from my mother's house. I had no place to stay, so Alex set me up in this condemned building over by where he lived. We got to be real good friends, and we would go out on a regular basis. We'd go out say around 10:30 at night and go to the park until around 11:30. From 11:30 until around 6:00 in the morning we were at the juice bar. At 6:00 he'd go to his house and I'd go either to the condemned apartment or to his house and sleep. I always waited until his mother would go to work. I would get something to eat and from around 3:00 on we just sat around the house and listened to music, and then just went out again as soon as 10:30 came around.

I didn't know that I was gay then. I knew something was different about me because I didn't go crazy when my friends would bring their fathers' *Playboy* magazines. At school they told me something was wrong with me. They said I was a fag. I didn't know what a fag was back then . . . I just knew that I was different. Once I moved in with my mother there were a lot more gays where she lived compared with where I was with my grandparents. There was just a whole lot of stuff going on and I started talking to my mother about what I was experiencing. Then my mom came out to me that she was a lesbian, and three or four months later I came out to her.

The main reason I came out to her was to get myself out of trouble for going out. I stayed out really late, or something like that, and she sat me down to talk about it. I kind of talked around it and then we started talking about gay stuff. I asked her what she would do if somebody else in the family said they were gay. She said she'd be happy for them, and I said something like, "Good; I'm gay." The punishment and everything was forgotten because it was such a shock for her. Maybe it wasn't a total shock . . . she always suspected 'cause I didn't do some of the things normal guys were doing. She knew but she didn't know. Part of it was like, well, wouldn't that be funny if he was and I was too. The question was always there and so when I came out to her she told me, "Well, why don't you come with me to the gay community center." They got me books and stuff to read. I had it a lot easier than the other guys because my mom was gay. It's a lot easier for her to understand what I'm going through and it's a lot easier for me to talk with her about what's going on.

She told me to stop going to the juice bar right around the time I met everyone. She found out the kind of people that went there. The crowd that's there are usually older people looking for younger kids—they call them chicken and chicken hawks. She was worried and I think she was embarrassed because some of her friends were going there too. She knew what these friends were like and they would come back and say, "I saw your son down at the juice bar." She told me to stop and I stopped for a while. But my friends still said, "Why don't you just come out with us . . . we want you to come out with us." So I started sneaking back out. She found out about it and a whole bunch of stuff happened.

Alex was the first person who introduced me to alcohol, that's how I got started. Once I got so drunk that I wound up in the hospital. It got to the point where my mother couldn't control me anymore because she didn't have the power to tell me you can't do this or that. If I want to do it, I'm going to do it anyway, even if she tells me, "I don't want you to do it." I'd know how she felt about it so I'd use that and I went out anyway. Finally the courts and the police and all this other stuff got brought into it. I ran away from home and I didn't have any place to go or anything, so I went to the park and Alex introduced me to prostitution. I never slept with anybody in the park but I used my age. I would get in the car and people would suspect that I was seventeen and I'd tell them that I was only fourteen. I told them, "If you don't give me so much money I'll call the cops on you for molesting a minor." I always brought them down by where I lived because it was right next to the police station.

Sometimes at night at late hours when I was drunk I would just sit on the bridge and let all the guys look at me till the cops got there. They found me there a couple of times. Once they see your face there a couple of times they know what you are doing there and they get to know you. They said if they saw me there again they would arrest me. But they found me there again and they didn't arrest me.

Another time my mother found me after I had been out all night. I came back home and my mother had to go to her AA meeting so she brought me with her. But I wasn't allowed in the meeting itself and the door was closed. I just snuck downstairs and went across the street to the park. The meeting was across the street from the park. I saw a friend who I hadn't seen in God knows how long. He asked me if I wanted to go out and I said yeah. I went back and asked my mother if I could spend the night at this friend's house. I tried to be slick and say, "Well, I think we need time away from each other," because we were getting mad at each other. She said, "No, I am not going to let you go out after you just stayed out all night last night." So, I ran away again that night. My mother called the cops and that's how I got involved with the runaway shelter. I don't know the whole story, but when I got back home she said, "I'm bringing you somewhere." She left me off at the runaway shelter.

At first, when I got there I kind of kept to myself because I was new and everything. Then it turned out to be good for me because it was like the family I never had. I basically had brothers and sisters and those were the best friends I had made since I had moved to this town. I wasn't really willing to work out any problems I had, but I had fun staying there because I liked the people there and it got to the point where I didn't want to go back home because I had such a good time there. It kept me out of a lot of trouble, the trouble I got into while I was living at home. I know if it could have gotten any worse it would have. Some of the stuff that I had done shocks me now when I look back on it. So I know if she hadn't taken me there, I don't know where I would be right now. I'm glad she did send me there even though I didn't get as much as I could have from being there. It was like I wasn't willing to work on my problems with the staff so I didn't. Being there kept me out of trouble for a while. I stayed there for a month and then I went back home because I thought that if I didn't, they would place me. I didn't really want to go back home but I didn't want to be placed so . . . I went back home. I had family counseling but I wasn't willing to work with it. At most of the meetings I just sat there and didn't say anything. After I had gotten out of the runaway shelter, I still went back there for counseling sessions.

I wanted to know what everybody was talking about, what's so big about alcohol. So I went out and I tried it for myself. Two other kids called me and asked me if I wanted to go out and I said, "Okay; where are we going?" And they said the Green Lion Pub, another gay bar, which I didn't know because I had never been in there. I asked them whether they knew what kind of bar it was. They said it was the only place that would serve minors. So we went there and some older guy liked me so he sat down with us and bought us drinks all night. He bought us rounds of beer and stuff like that, and then we moved on from there to pure alcohol, to Alabama Slammers, which are supposed to have five different kinds of alcohol in them. I was drunk, but if we had gone straight home I would have made it home.

After we left there we were planning on going back home, but Rachel was drunk and decided she wanted to go uptown and beat some girl up. So we get to some house and they tell me to wait outside. It started to rain outside so I moved onto the porch. I was sitting on the stairs and I remember telling myself that, "Boy, you are going to throw up." I started to throw up and I didn't want to throw up on their porch so I made it outside. I just kept throwing up and throwing up and whenever I felt like throwing up I just opened my mouth and it came out. Finally they came back out and I said I was sick. They thought that I was playing around but they were smashed too and they didn't pay much attention. They started walking down the street and I couldn't. I managed to get up but I was leaning on them and we started walking down the street and I just collapsed on the sidewalk. They left because they thought I was joking. I don't know if they made it home or what, but I was woken up by the ambulance and they asked me if I had been smoking pot and I said no, and they said did you have too much to drink and I said yeah. They took me to the hospital where I stayed overnight. I found out what had happened, that I had passed out in front of some kid's house who called the cops and the ambulance because he was looking out the window. He said he saw a car full of people come by and he thought I got thrown out so he called the ambulance and then called the cops. I don't know what happened. I remember seeing the girls walk away and then the next thing I remember the ambulance and the fire trucks and the cops and all these people were around me. Then they brought me to Saint Charles Hospital, pumped my stomach, and called my mother. The next day they called a taxi for me and I went home.

Then I got sent back to the runaway shelter. At the runaway shelter I was comfortable because I didn't really have to work on any of my problems if I didn't choose to. They didn't force me to so I didn't. Then I went back home, but I didn't want to be there, so I went back to the runaway shelter. The runaway shelter sent me back home again and then my next step was the detox center.

From there they sent me to some holding shelter. At that shelter I wasn't worried about my problems . . . I was more worried about keeping myself safe. It was in an area that was very strange. This shelter is basically a holding place until they find a place to put you. The place was terrible. They took all your clothes and gave you four changes. You couldn't carry anything in your pocket except your comb and everything was locked up. I talked to my mother about once a week. They only allow you one phone call a week. Everybody had a certain day they could talk to their parents. When holidays came around, the workers didn't want to be there. They wanted to spend the holidays with their families so they got rid of all the kids. They would call the parents up and ask them if they could bring them home. If there was any kids left over they would bring them to their house or find some place to bring them so they could spend time with their families. They weren't suppose to do that because you weren't suppose to have any contact with anybody. It's like ten miles away from anywhere.

After a while it was kind of okay because I started to get on the good side of staff. I wrote a letter to one of my friends and I was talking about myself being gay. Some of the guys found the letter and the staff brought me down into the office and gave me this lecture about how I couldn't sleep with other people here and stuff like that. Then I started running into other hassles with some of the kids. The two guys who found the letter told everybody else in the house. So everybody knew about me and I had a hard time with that. The staff didn't really say nothing about it except for this one guy whose nephew was in the shelter too and he would always pick on me about it. So I decided to go back to public school, rather than go to school there; that way I won't have to deal with it. But that didn't work out because I had missed so much school—they didn't know where I belonged. So then I went back to school at the shelter and it was a lot easier. I was too lazy to get up and go somewhere else so I went there.

Then some kid came, I don't even remember his name. One day when the rest of the kids were all on rec we were playing pool and stuff like that. This kid said he wanted to sleep with me. I said, "No, I don't want to do that." I just went through a whole bunch of stuff with that and it got to a point where he wasn't asking anymore, he was trying to force me, so I went to talk to the staff about it. I never had sex with him, he never physically forced me, but like when I went upstairs he was already there, waiting in my room. He had a different room than mine and him and his roommate weren't getting along. They switched him and put him in my room. I had to go through all this stuff around that so I went to staff about it and they said okay, we will do something about it. But they didn't really do nothing about it. The kid was still bothering me until the day I left. There was just a whole bunch of stuff going around the shelter. I don't like to think about the holding shelter as much as I like to think about the runaway shelter because I had some great times there. I was originally supposed to be there for two or three weeks. But then my hearing got changed to December 15 so I was there until I went to court. Court sent me back to the holding shelter 'cause I didn't have an interview for the placement.

The court gave me another two or three weeks, and they were just waiting for an opening up here. I went to court and met up again with Alex and Julie who were also at the courthouse. During this time they had had a baby. They were going to court because Julie's mother was trying to take the baby from Alex and Julie because Julie was unfit. I saw them afterwards and we were sitting there talking about old times. The court finally told me that they were going to place me for a year. I was, like, if I'm going to get placed for a year, I'm going to go out and have one weekend of fun before I get placed. So my probation officer, who I think is stupid, tells me to wait right here and he would go get the car and take me back to the shelter. After I found out I'm going to get placed for a year, I left with Alex and Julie. They told me how they got this house and everything now so I stayed there. I don't remember how long but I stayed there and they stayed out for a while. Then I called the runaway shelter and I found out that the holding shelter had called the runaway shelter and told them to be on the lookout for me. I think maybe two days later I was planning on going out again but I didn't want to because my pants were black and I felt like a grub. So I called the runaway shelter and told them I wanted to come back. I don't remember how I got down there; I think I walked. I went into the supermarket with Alex and Julie's friend and I called them from there. I went to the runaway shelter's independent living apartment, where Frank is still living. Frank was talking to some-body down there, I don't remember who. He told them that he saw me the night before at Dunkin Donuts, 'cause I saw him down there. He said if I needed a place to stay I could stay at his place. I didn't want to call my mother because I just didn't want to deal with that. So I called the runaway shelter and they brought me back up the day before I was supposed to go to court. I knew that I was getting placed because they had already told me, but some man at the shelter had me worried about it because he wouldn't let me pack my bags. They thought for sure I was coming back. So I went to court again and for some reason, I don't know why, the part about me running away the last time didn't get brought up by the judge. The law guardian asked me where I had been and I just told him that I went out with my friends and he says okay. Then I think that was the time he asked me if my mom was a lesbian. He brought me upstairs and said, "I have a few questions to ask you. You know you're getting placed?" and I said, "Yeah." He said, "I just want to ask you one thing: is your mother a lesbian?" I said, "What do you mean a lesbian?" I was playing dumb, I knew what a lesbian was and I knew if she was or not, but he asked me and I don't know what he was asking for so I said, "I don't know." He said, "Does she ever bring women home or girlfriends home?" I said, "No, not to my knowledge." He said, "Okay, fine," and he brought me back downstairs. We were in and out just like that and my mother was there. She came upstairs with me and we were waiting for my probation officer to come back in and sign out a car and bring me back up to my new placement.

Mom and I weren't having much contact any more. It was out of her hands now. There was nothing she could do so a lot of anger was put aside. We were just dealing with now. She tried to be there for me and stuff like that.

I was placed after violating probation. Fran brought me here to the group home. It seemed to be real nice and during the day Marc and some other counselor were there. It was okay when I first got here 'cause there was only one other kid in the house. I said I was just going to keep myself clean and then it turned out the other kid wanted to sleep with me. I went through all this shit with him, it was really bad. The kid did say that we slept together and I said, "Why would I want to sleep with you?" This was just after I had left the holding shelter with this other guy that wanted to sleep with me. This situation was a lot worse than the kid in the holding shelter because there they kept their eye on you a lot more than the group home. I was sitting there in my room with my stuff and he comes in and sits down and says, "Do you want to talk? Come in and we will play cards or something like that." So when they started cleaning my room I went in there and we played some stupid game. He started telling me about this other kid that had lived at the group home before, and the kid he was talking about was really himself. He was telling me that they have had kids that have gotten in trouble and come back and they had done such and such with other guys. I was like, really? . . . and he was, like, yeah . . . and there was even rumors about this kid sucking this kid off, and I knew it was him. Then a counselor came upstairs and said I wasn't supposed to be in there. I went back to my room.

He wouldn't knock when he came into my room, he just came right in. Sometimes he would walk right in and I wasn't dressed so I asked him if he would knock before he came in. He said okay. It started getting a lot worse. He spent most of his time on restriction because he was always going off, so by the time I was going upstairs he would already be in bed. One time I came upstairs and he called me into his room and I came in to see what he wanted. He was jerking off and it was like he was doing it to get my attention 'cause he wanted me to sleep with him, and I looked at him and said, "Yeah?" He said, "I just wanted to say good night," and I said, "Okay, good night," and I walked out of his room and closed the door. He came into my room and he was like, why won't you sleep with me? I said, "Because I'm not attracted to you." He said, "It's because you don't like me," and I said, "No, it's not 'cause I don't like you, it's just that I don't like you in that way." He said, "You were in other relationships," and I told him that I was in one other relationship. He asked me if I slept with the person, and I told him that I don't really think that is any of his business. But I did, and I was too young to realize what I was doing. Again he said, "Well, why won't you sleep with me when you know you can do it on a regular basis." I told him that I wasn't attracted to him and that I didn't like him in that way and he just couldn't take no for an answer.

Finally I was talking to the psychiatrist there, and I told her about it. This was a little bit later, but I talked to her about it and then stuff started getting done about it. He finally got discharged from the house but before he left it was a lot better. More kids started coming into the house. I had a roommate, and it even got up to like four or five kids there. It was fine during the week but then when the weekend came I wasn't on home visit like the rest of the kids. Me and my mother weren't to that point in our relationship yet. It ended up being me and him at home again. We would go out and do stuff and he would be in this really good mood and I'd get worried because I knew, oh shit, he was going to try something on me. Finally he left and a whole bunch of other kids came and in and out. There had been like three different households since I have been there.

Then I started going back to the park. I can't remember what month it was. What had happened was when I was AWOL one time I was in the park with a friend of mine. I was supposed to meet some friends and this guy came over to me. He said, "You might think I'm a little crazy for coming over and saying this but I really like you, and maybe we should get together." I told him I was AWOL from a group home, hoping that would scare him off because that was the first time someone younger actually approached me. I didn't know what to do and he said, "Oh, really; well, I can take care of everything. I have friends and they will find us a place to stay." So I was just talking to him, and I started walking away and he started following me. He said, "I'm going to go out and make us some money," because he was a prostitute. I wasn't doing that stuff anymore and he tried to become my pimp. He tried to sell me off to these people and he was, like, won't you go over and do that guy, I know he pays good. Again I told him I don't do that stuff, and he was, like, "Okay, I'll make money for both of us." He says, "So when will I be able to see you again?" and I said, "I don't know." He said, "I heard you say you were going over to the juice bar with some friends," and I said that I was and he wanted to know what the juice bar was. I told him that it's just this bar I go to and he told me maybe he'll see me over there and I said okay. I didn't think the guy knew where it was so I went over there. He comes in and nobody else that I knew was in there so the guy comes over and he starts talking to me. Then my friend Donald came in and even though we really didn't know each other that well, I was so scared, I went up to him and said, "Donald, you have got to help me. Make believe that we are seeing each other so this guy will leave me alone." So Donald played along. He asked me if I was ready to go home and I said, "Yeah." The guy asked if we were lovers. Donald told him we were. The guy asked, "When did you two meet?" Donald said, "Tonight." The guy thought that I was just going home with him for the night and I was just doing it for money. He was expecting me to come back and so he said, "Will I see you back here?" and I said, "Yeah." He asked about when and I said that I probably wouldn't be back until three or four o'clock in the morning.

So me and Donald went and rode all over the place. He was going to bring me back to the group home, but I decided I didn't want to come back home 'cause I liked Donald. He was a really nice person. We started talking and we got lost on the highway 'cause we were so into the conversation. We spent like an hour trying to find our way back to the group home but we wound up back in downtown, so we went back to the juice bar. The guy was gone. We got some coffee, sat and talked and we had a lot of things in common. I wound up staying at Donald's house for like three days, but we didn't sleep together or anything like that. It was just like the beginning of the relationship. He didn't know at first that I lived in a group home (I had told him where I lived but not that it was a group home). I had sort of a semirelationship with Donald and we started doing a whole bunch of stuff that I couldn't continue doing because I was in a group home. Pretty soon all this stuff was just going to start coming in and so that basically ended before it really got started. We are friends and stuff now.

Meanwhile that other guy was mad because he was waiting at the juice bar until three o'clock in the morning and I didn't show up. I saw the guy the next night and he was, like, "You did me wrong." I said, "How did I do you wrong?" He said, "You told me you were going to be back here at three o'clock." I said, "Well, I was here at three o'clock." I was praying that he wasn't there at three o'clock and it turned out that he was. I said, "Well, I was here at three o'clock and you weren't here so I left." He said, "Okay, so are you two lovers now?" And I said, "Yeah, you can say that." He was pissed off about that and he talked to a cop. He gave the cop my description and told him that I was carrying a knife or some sort of a weapon and that I was a prostitute. He said that I seemed like I was in a whole mess of trouble. He knew damn well I wasn't carrying a knife, and he knew I didn't like him and that I didn't want to do anything with him. He was pissed off about what I did with him; that's why he talked to the cop.

When I got back to to the group home I realized I could make $230 for my time and still get allowance and not have to do nothing for it. I mean it was like, wow, I could basically get all the clothes I wanted, because I love clothes. So I continued to do it a while after I was in the group home. I would sign out and go downtown and do this stuff. I was getting a lot of money from the guys. I mean it was easy money and it kept me warm and it kept my stomach full but I never really turned a trick. I never ever slept with anything that came out of the park because I was worried about disease and all that stuff. The most that happened was this guy put his hand right there and he realized that once he put his hand there nothing was going to happen. I would look out the window and I never looked at them. Most of the times I got in the cars I didn't say nothing and they would get really psyched and ask if I had a place around there. I would memorize their license plate number and I'd bring them downtown. It was right next to the police station and you would think that they would think something but they didn't. After they found out nothing was going to go on they would kick me out of the car. I would get out of the car and then before they pulled away I would scare them. I'd say, "Right over there is the police station and I have your name, description, and your license number. If you don't give me such and such amount of money then I'm going to go to the police and give them this information and tell them you molested a minor." Ninety-nine percent of the time it worked. I had one guy that drove off, he didn't care, but all the others did what I wanted them to do.

One guy told me he was a cop. He wasn't a cop because if he was, he wouldn't be in the park, even if he was off duty. After you go there for such a length of time you know what cars the cops drive and you know where the cops are. The only time I really ran into anything is when the guy said he was a cop and he tried to scare me off by taking out his wallet and he was going to pull out his badge. I said, "Well, while you are doing that you can take out a twenty-dollar bill too." I didn't believe he was a cop so he ended up giving me forty dollars instead of twenty because I said I really was going to tell the cops on you anyway. He said, "Wait, here is another twenty bucks. Just don't tell them."

The way I am I just can't go out and have sex with anybody. It's against what I am for and I feel sorry for people that have to use the people that are out there such as myself for their personal enjoyment. The people that go to the park, it's like they go to the park as soon as the lights go out. I don't like to go to the park after the lights go out because I know what goes on in those hills. During the day the park is for everybody but once it gets dark out they know what goes on in the park. It's just up until recently that the police have really started to crack down. There used to be long lines going out of the park and cops would occasionally come by and everyone would pull away. Then the cops would come back in another three hours and the cars would just come right back in after the cops were gone. If someone told on me I could just as easy tell on the next person as they could tell on me. And it's like, what were you doing in the park anyway? . . . How would you know? So no one is really going to say anything unless it was a cop telling you he was going to put you in jail; that's the only way.

Eventually the group home caught on. My counselor said she was going to have to violate me for my AWOL. She said she didn't know what that would mean and what the judge was going to do to me. So I got scared, but she said, "If you can show them that you will stop all this stuff, things might be okay." So they brought in this very cool cop to talk to me. After I had the talk with the cop, all that just stopped. I still go to the park but it's for totally different reasons now. I go there now with a group of friends and we bring a radio and we sit there and we dance and stuff like that. We just go and hang out and we talk and it's funny because now people come up to me and ask me if I want to make some money. We laugh about it because people have the nerve to come up to us and ask us, when just a few months ago I was the one that was going up to people. When older guys are coming up to me now and ask us if we want to make fifty bucks and we will say no. If they will try again we will say no, no, no, and we laugh about it now.

I think I'll go back home to my mom's when I leave here. She just met her tenth anniversary of sobriety. I want to become a child care worker. I know I need to go to college for that. I worry about what it's going to be like when I get out there. It's not going to be the same . . . it isn't going to be two or three people around all the time . . . there was always someone to talk to here. My mother has her stuff to do. Hopefully I'll be able to help myself and not be so dependent on other people to help me through my problems.

I haven't thought about any relationships much. The last relationship I had, nothing was wrong with it, but I'm just starting to find really, really good friends. I'm just taking it all a step at a time. It's funny because I do want a family. I think I will be able to and if I am still gay then I would adopt if I was secure.

The message that my grandparents always gave me was that we didn't have to do this for you. They didn't have to adopt me because I could be someplace else. That was the only reason I felt bad up to a point about some of the stuff that I was doing. It is true they didn't have to do it and I finally told them that I didn't have any say in the matter. I still see my grandparents once in a while . . . mostly holidays and stuff like that.

I think when kids are in trouble like I was, it's really important to get help as soon as possible. You can't run away from your problems because it is just going to hurt you more in the long run. The people here at the group home have been really helpful. They didn't let me slack like I was used to doing. I was used to getting away with a whole mess of stuff, but they always called me on my stuff. They let me know what you can do and they were fair in a way that I could understand and deal with so it really helped. I used to think that everybody else had the power in the situation but I finally realized that I have a lot of power and I can control a lot of the things that go on in my life. It's not one-sided anymore. I do have some input and knowing that really helps a lot.

Sasha
(nineteen years old)

I know very little about what was going on for my parents when I was born. They already had one son, my brother Tim, who's a couple of years older. My mom was in her twenties when she had me, and she was with my father. I was the first girl, and two others would soon follow, so there were four of us kids altogether. We had a large extended family, at least on my father's side; there were tons of local relatives—all New Yorkers. My mother's family is from South Carolina, and they're scattered all over the place, but none are in New York. My dad's relatives dislike my mom, and that makes me dislike them, 'cause I love my mother . . . and if anyone tries to turn me against her I think I'll try and kill them.

My dad had always worked as a janitor at the school, pretty steadily, although he changed schools a couple of times. Mom didn't work during those early years—she took care of us kids—but today she works.

I really don't remember much at all about my early childhood. I do know that we didn't have much money when I was growing up. I was pretty close with my brothers and sisters. Me and my younger sister used to do the most devilish things and my brother always told on us. But as we got older, me and my brother, we got closer to each other.

One thing I do remember very well is that my father drank a lot, and got real abusive. He used to beat my mother when he got drunk. I used to see it, and it hurt me a lot. I felt so helpless, I just would scream, cry, and hide in my room. I couldn't bear seeing my mother being beat on like that. Mom would threaten to leave him, and say she was packing her things and taking the kids away forever . . . but she never did. They would always make up and then the same thing would happen all over again. Dad mainly got violent when he was drunk. Other people were aware of his drinking problems, like the neighbors knew everything. So did my aunts and other relatives, 'cause I used to run and go get my aunt sometimes and tell her what was going on. She'd run back to the house with me and try to stop it, and sometimes the police would have to come over. One time, the police actually had my father removed from the house for a couple of days. I was about seven at the time.

My father was violent with all of us really, he was pretty much a violent person. He used to have these really bad violent outbursts and one time even went to jail for shooting a gun at somebody. He used to beat me with tree branches which left welts all over my body. I used to be really scared of him. I cried a lot. There was nothing I could do. Sometimes he would just slap me up against the wall, and bang my head over and over again. I tried to figure out what I had done wrong to deserve these beatings. Sometimes it happened when I made a little mistake, like I broke a glass by accident, he'd think I did it on purpose. Which wasn't fair at all, 'cause you know, as I got older, I learned that everyone makes mistakes and accidents happen. But I don't think I deserved these beatings. My mother tried to stop him, but she was pretty much scared of him. He'd tell her to shut up and get out. He basically had control over all of us, because back then he was the main provider and we were all dependent upon him. I think that's why my mother was really scared to leave him. She had no way of taking care of us, and if she were forced to go back home to her mother, my grandmother was not in a situation to take care of us either—she was hurting financially too.

Things starting getting really bad for me when I was thirteen. My father began beating me with sticks and stuff for no reason. At times I felt like he was going to beat my brains out, and I decided that I wasn't going to take it anymore. That's when I started running away from home. You know, everything wasn't his fault, I did some things, and contributed, but I don't think that what I did deserved that treatment. So one day I ran away to a relative's house, to my aunt's. She didn't tell my father where I was 'cause she knew what was going on and that I would really get it if he found me. After a couple of days, I went to a friend's house. Well, that's when my mother told the police I was missing. So when the police caught up with me they took me to the police station and asked me a lot of questions, like whether I wanted to go home that night. I begged them not to send me back home. They put me in a temporary foster home, and then my mother filed a PINS petition to make sure I'd be taken care of.

After a while I got out of the temporary foster home and went home, hoping that maybe things were going to work out this time. But they didn't. When I got home, we all were supposed to be in family counseling, but only me and my mother went; my father refused to attend.

I used to come to school with my arms swollen and all bruised up, and people asked me what was going on. I told them that I fell and they didn't believe me and started asking all kinds of questions, like whether my parents abused me. I lied and said no. I don't know why I lied; I guess I was scared to tell, scared for me and for him, what would happen and stuff. One time, someone saw my father hitting me at the school; I must have been about fourteen. He was beating me in the car and one of my teachers called protective services on him. Someone ended up coming to our house. My father thought that I told, but I hadn't told. And he kept asking me questions, and the workers were asking me questions, and at first I said no, that my father didn't hit me. But then I said yes, he did—you know, I just came out with the truth. And I sat there and thought, well, maybe I can get some kind of help and maybe my father can get some kind of help. I don't remember what happened, all I know was that I was removed from the home.

None of my other brothers or sisters got involved in this stuff—that is, ran away, or got in trouble. I don't know why, maybe 'cause I'm very sensitive. You know, I mean, you can say some of the littlest things and they can hurt my feelings. And at that point in time I felt, well, they don't love me, they don't need me, so just let me go, you know, that's how I felt. I also felt unloved 'cause they didn't believe me when I told them that my uncle had sexually abused me. I was about fourteen. They thought about it and everything, they were, like, maybe she's telling the truth, but I don't think so. So I took it a step further, and told the psychologist I was seeing, which led to my uncle having to go to court. That's when I ran away again, to get away from my uncle, and I was put in a foster home.

I was in and out of lots of places—group homes, temporary foster homes, maybe twenty of them within a couple of years. Sometimes I would just go into the foster home, you know, or I would talk to my parents or whatever, go back to court, and then they would send me home and we would try again to make it work. I don't know why they kept switching me so much. I was getting tired of it, getting switched from school to school, you know, I couldn't get used to any of it. I'm the type of person who gets very close to people just like that, you know, and I used to get close to people and didn't want to leave. One time I asked a woman at one of my group homes if she would adopt me. I said, "Please adopt me," and I just held her and wouldn't let her go. It seemed like every time I turned around the courts were putting me someplace else. I don't know why they moved me so much, like in some foster homes there is a time limit, you know, up to a certain period of time you can stay; maybe they just wanted to see how things would work out. I never asked the courts to stop moving me around. I kept my mouth shut most of the time, just like I used to do at home. I was very, very quiet, but I was very violent too. Yes, I was. When I was upset, when somebody would say something to me I didn't like I would beat them up. That's how violent I was. I got into lots of fights, and took out my anger on them.

I ran away from a lot of group homes. They took me to a new place, and I used to run and the cops would put me back there and I'd run again. I didn't run as much from my foster homes, some of them, when I felt uncomfortable. It wasn't the easiest time of my life. I started smoking cigarettes a lot, and picked up drinking too. There were plenty of times when I thought of ending it all. I thought, oh, God, why did you put me on earth to go through all this, I don't deserve to go through all of this. But then, I would think—well, suicide would go through my mind and then I would tell myself to fight it. Keep fighting the urge to hurt myself, and fight to keep myself together as a whole person. I was depressed a lot, always depressed. Sometimes when I got depressed it wasn't so bad, but I was always depressed. Always. I'd cry a lot, and I'd sing to make myself feel better, to try to take my mind off things.

One night, I was at the group home, and I got real upset about something. I exploded, I was so angry, and made a big hole in the wall. I got real violent and then ran way. That's when they knew they had to do something drastic with me. I think that they thought, we've got to stop this girl from running away, we got to do something. So they sent me upstate to a school that was kind of like a detention center for runaways and kids who get in trouble. It was a big place, for kids like me, you know, that couldn't keep still. It was a good place for me and helped me a lot. It made me wake up to a lot of things and realize that I couldn't keep beating up on people and trying to harm myself. There was this one lady there, she was very nice and she took a lot of time out with me. She made me realize that I couldn't keep doing certain things, that there was no way I could remain in society if I did. You know, if I try to kill myself then they will put me in a mental hospital and if I hurt somebody really bad and kill them then I will go to jail. She helped me to see that I had choices and said, "I hope you choose them wisely." I've always had a lot of counseling, 'cause I need someone to talk to a lot. I always need that. The restrictions also made me think too. They made me think about what I did and why I got into a situation. I loved school there. It helped having the boys around—I had about four or five boyfriends in the two years that I was there. I also learned how to deal with street kids.

So, after about two years, they felt that I was ready for society again, but they didn't want to place me right back home. They felt maybe, you know, things might not go right at home so they better put me in a group home where I could make home visits. I really hated to leave the school and cried; it was the longest place I'd been and it felt like home. I stayed at that group home for about a year, until I turned eighteen, and prepared for my GED exam and worked at a fast-food restaurant.

Then I went home. My father ranted and raved that he wanted me home. They weren't going to let me go, and wanted me to make a couple of long home visits, but he said, "No, I want her home. Everything's going to be fine." Well, everything went smoothly at first—for a while. But then it started up all over again. He started coming down on me again. My brother told me to ignore him, that he did it to everyone. I told my mother I wasn't going to put up with it. You know, 'cause I don't have to live like this anymore. But I put up with it for a while. I said nothing, kept my mouth shut, and went into my room and listened to music. My father wasn't hitting Mom anymore, because my brother now was old enough to beat him up. The older we got, the more he laid off of beating us up, but he and my mom still get to it to this day, he always says to her, "Well, you can leave and take the rest of the kids with you 'cause I don't want to be bothered with you," stuff like that.

I don't think my father ever got help; he might have and I don't know about it. But he was religious. It was mandatory for us to go to church every Sunday and before we went to church we had to sit up in front of the TV at seven o'clock in the morning when I wanted to get some sleep and watch the reverend. It was on channel eleven and then after that my father would quiz us on it so I thought a lot about church. I liked singing in the choir, I loved that part. I know what my religion is but I don't follow most of the rules, but, you know, I'm going to start. 'Cause I feel God has a big part to do with my life. Without God, I feel lost. 'Cause I feel he's been helping me and keeping me together all these years. I could have stayed in the gutter somewhere, you know, or something could have happened to me . . . he saved me all those times. And I think I owe it to him.

I lasted at home for a few months. For a while, I sat there and tried to ignore him, but then I started thinking of telling him off, and how I felt about his doing certain things, and what that would be like. I started having a pretty bad drinking problem, and reached for the bottle a lot, like this was going to solve my problems. Every time me and my father would get into it I would just go to his bar, you know, and I would always make comments to my sister, disregard what I'm doing, don't do this. Don't be like me and drink away your problems. 'Cause my sisters look up to me a lot and I just want to show them that regardless of what I've been through, or if they should happen to go through the same thing, you can come out a winner in the end, there is a life for you. It's your life and you can make something of yourself—that's what I'm going to show my little sisters, you know. I care about them a lot and I don't want anything to happen to them and I want the best for them in life, even my brother. Then my father would say, "You just get out of our house or pay support. You don't like my rules, then out." He kicked me out anyway, eventually. He got tired of me and told me he didn't care what happened to me, I could go out on the streets and be a prostitute and it wouldn't bother him, he just wanted me out of his house.

What did I do? I went to stay with a friend for a few days, and then I stayed with my uncle. Then my uncle left me with this guy because he went away. This guy tried to force me to have sex with him, in order to stay in the house, but even though I had no place to go, had no home, no money, and no place to sleep, I didn't want to stoop that low. That night, when he was trying to get me to stay at his house for sex, I walked around all night. I had a key to the house so when he left for work the next morning, I went back and started making phone calls to runaway hotlines. And then someone from this program came and got me. The main priority was trying to find a place for me to stay. First she was going to send me to a shelter, but I got up enough guts—well, she helped me get up enough guts to call my best friend Susan who lives a few towns away. This counselor also gave me some money, and tokens for traveling. So I went to Susan's house and it was fine. We had so much fun until she started getting jealous. She didn't like the fact that her mom started paying more attention to me than to her. I sat down and talked to her and tried to let her know that she's her daughter and her mother will always love her. But I left, even though we're still in touch, and she tells me to this day that she feels bad that she was jealous, and said she was being selfish, that she didn't want to share her mommy. I said, "I don't blame you, I wouldn't want to share my mommy either."

From Susan's house, I applied to get into this independent living program, where I'm currently living. I had to go through screening tests which asked me all kinds of questions, like what I wanted to do with my life. The final decision was made after they set up a dinner date where I went to the house and ate dinner with the girls and just got introduced. They showed me around and I got a feel for the place. Then I moved in, and it's been great. I've learned quite a few other things about myself here that they are pointing out to me, things I didn't quite understand about myself, I'm making new connections. I've tried to understand them and do something about it.

Someday, I'd like to go to college! I want to go to college so bad. I am so excited 'cause I like mixing with a lot of kids and everything in the classrooms. When I went back home, after being gone for so long, I went to a business school for a while. I just loved it! I loved the feeling of just being there with other classmates—I don't know why, but I just loved doing homework and being normal. Leading a normal life. I loved it. And that's another reason why I'm looking forward to going to college. I'll be around a whole bunch of people. It will be a good experience.

I have my drinking under control now. I kind of got it from my father actually, although I didn't want to admit it at first. But then I sat down and just reviewed a couple of things. "Here you go," I said to myself. "Sasha, you can't do this 'cause you will end up just like him if not worse." I knew if I didn't stop I'd either end up hurting somebody or myself, catching a liver disease or something. I didn't quit right away. I took a couple of drinks at a time, or when I got upset I tried to limit myself. And I swear, I'm never touching another drink again. I can't, I'm scared to . . . *No. No. No.* I will not. And I have one more nasty habit to get rid of: cigarettes. But I can do it. I can do the impossible. That's how I feel now about my life, because of all this stuff I've been through, I know I can do the impossible. I will set very high expectations for myself and reach them. Not right away, depending on what they are within a period of time, but I will get there sooner or later. I've got a lot of goals for myself; I want to be an executive secretary, and I also want to sing. If my singing career turns out right, I won't need to do the secretary stuff, but if it doesn't I'll just play around with it.

I want to put the past behind me and start anew, and never go back home. No, no, no, no! I won't forget it, I'll never forget it because it is constantly on my mind. But I can put it aside and try to work things out.

I don't think I'll ever start a family, and I don't want to get married. I can make it by myself; that's the way I want to do it. I might have one child, just one, and raise her all by myself. I don't think I'm going to need a man. I do know that I would never do to my child what my family did to me. Never. I would try to be more reasonable, when a child gets to be thirteen or fourteen and they want to hang out. I'll be kind of lenient. Maybe if my child wants to go to a movie, or something, I'll come pick her up from the movies, you know, stuff like that. I would just try to be the best parent, and I'd love my child. Because of what I've been through I would try not to make those mistakes. If I do make any of those mistakes, I would try to do something about them.

I fantasize a lot about meeting up with a little girl who is in the same situation that I was in, and she runs away from home and bumps into me on the street. I pick her up and tell her to let her parents know that she is okay. But then I raise her. I'd raise her to the best of my ability and stay with her because I have been through those things. Some people might not understand her, but I would. I would be very patient and work on that trust until I knew she was ready to go. And I'd give special help to her and explain that she wasn't the only person in this predicament right now. There are many other kids out there in the world going through the same thing and I'd tell her I've been through it. Maybe some of my past experiences could help.

I think it is really important to let parents know that when they kick a child out of their house, you never know what's going to happen. I could have ended it last June, or I could have ended up having to steal for a living. Thank God I didn't have to but there are kids out there doing that now, and when I see those young prostitutes on TV, I feel so sad.

'Cause they could live at home. If parents would try to reach out to their children—because it's a different day and age and things don't work the way they did back then, and if they have problems they should just reach out to help, because in one way they will come out on top. I hope that people can learn from my story.

Notes

Chapter 1. Maltreatment among Runaway and Homeless Youth

1. See U.S. Department of Health and Human Services, *Runaway and Homeless Youth National Program Inspection,* Office of The Inspector General, Oct. 1983; National Network of Runaway and Youth Services, "Preliminary Findings from the National Network's Survey of Runaway and Homeless Youth." Testimony before the U.S. House of Representatives Subcommittee on Human Resources, Jan. 29, 1988.

2. R.L. Jenkins, "The Runaway Reaction," *American Journal of Psychiatry* 128(1971):168–73; American Psychiatric Association, *Diagnostic and Statistical Manual of Mental Disorders,* 2d ed. (Washington, D.C.: American Psychiatric Association, 1968).

3. M. Janus, A. McCormack, A. Burgess, and C. Hartman, *Adolescent Runaways: Causes and Consequences* (Lexington, Mass.: Lexington Books, 1987).

4. T. Brennan, D. Huizinga, and D. Elliott, *The Social Psychology of Runaways* (Lexington, Mass.: Lexington Books, 1978).

5. J. Gordon and M. Beyer, *Runaways and Community Mental Health* (Washington D.C.: U.S. Department of Health and Human Services, DHHS Publication No. ADM 81-955, 1981).

6. Janus et al., *Adolescent Runaways.*

7. See National Network of Runaway and Youth Services, "Preliminary Findings"; J. Garbarino, J. Wilson, and A. Garbarino, "The Adolescent Runaway," in *Troubled Youth, Troubled Families,* ed. J. Garbarino, C. Schellenbach, and J. Sebes (New York: Aldine Publishers, 1986); E. Farber, C. Kinast, W.D. McCoard, and D. Falkner, "Violence in Families of Adolescent Runaways," *Child Abuse and Neglect* 8 (1984):295–99.

8. S. Gutierres and J. Reich, "A Developmental Perspective on Runaway Behavior: Its Relationship to Child Abuse," *Child Abuse and Neglect* 60 (1981):89–94.

9. Farber, Kinast, McCoard, and Falkner, "Violence in Families of Adolescent Runaways."

10. See A. Burgess, M. Janus, A. McCormack, and J. Wood, "Canadian Runaways: Youth in Turmoil and Running for Their Lives" (Paper presented at Symposium on Street Youth, Toronto, 1986); C. Adams-Tucker, "Proximate Effects of Sexual Abuse In Childhood: A Report on 28 Children," *American Journal of Psychiatry* 139 (1982); R. Young, W. Godfrey, B. Mathews, and G. Adams, "Runaways: A Review of Negative Consequences," *Family Relations* 32 (1983):275–81.

11. National Network of Runaway and Youth Services, "Preliminary Findings."

12. I. Lourie, P. Campiglia, L. James, and J. Dewitt, "Adolescent Abuse and Neglect: The Role of Runaway Youth Programs," *Children Today* 8 (1979):27–40; D. Shaffer and C. Caton, *Runaway and Homeless Youth in New York City: A Report to the Ittleson Foundation.* (New York: Division of Child Psychiatry, New York State Psychiatric Institute and Columbia University College of Physicians and Surgeons, 1984); P. Nilson, "Psychological Profiles of Runaway Children and Adolescents," in *Self-destructive Behavior in Children and Adolescents,* ed. C.F. Wells and I.R. Stuart (New York: Van Nostrand Reinhold, 1981).

13. K. Libertoff, "Runaway children and social network interaction." (Paper presented at the meetings of the American Psychological Association, Washington, D.C., 1976).

14. Garbarino, Wilson, and Garbarino, "The Adolescent Runaway."

15. See M. Cohen, *Identifying and Combating Juvenile Prostitution* (Tulsa, Okla.: National Resource Center for Youth Services, 1987); M. Silbert and A. Pines, "Sexual Child Abuse as an Antecedent to Prostitution," *Child Abuse and Neglect* 5 (1981):407–11.

16. Young et al., "Runaways: A Review."

17. Janus et al., *Adolescent Runaways.*

18. Burgess et al., "Canadian Runaways."

19. L. Olson, E. Liebow, F. Mannino, and M. Shore, "Runaway Children Twelve Years Later: A Follow-up," *Journal of Family Issues* 1 (1980):165–88.

Chapter 2. Adolescent Maltreatment: Definition and Understanding

1. M. Ziefert, "Abuse and Neglect: The Adolescent as Hidden Victim," in *Social Work with Abused and Neglected Children,* ed. Kathleen Coulborn Faller (New York: Free Press, 1980).

2. C. Kempe, F. Silverman, and B. Steele, "The Battered Child Syndrome," *Journal of the American Medical Association* 181 (1962):17–24.

3. B. Fisher and J. Berdie, "Adolescent Abuse and Neglect: Issues of Incidence, Intervention, and Service Delivery," *Child Abuse and Neglect* 2 (1978):173–92.

4. Fisher and Berdie, "Adolescent Abuse and Neglect."

5. See J. Berdie and S. Wexler, "Preliminary Research on Selected Adolescent Maltreatment Issues: An Analysis of Supplemental Data from the Four Ado-

lescent Maltreatment Projects," in *Adolescent Maltreatment Issues and Program Models* (Washington, D.C.: DHHS Publication No. [OHDS] 84-30339, 1980); B. Fisher, J. Berdie, J. Cook, and N. Day, *Adolescent Abuse and Neglect: Intervention Strategies.* (Washington, D.C.: DHHS Publication No. [OHDS] 80-30266, 1980).

6. P. Libbey and R. Bybee, "The Physical Abuse of Adolescents," *Journal of Social Issues* 35 (1979):101–26.

7. U.S. Department of Health and Human Services, *Study Findings: National Study of the Incidence and Severity of Child Abuse and Neglect* (Washington, D.C.: National Center on Child Abuse and Neglect, DHHS Publication No. [OHDS] 81-80325, 1981).

8. American Association for Protecting Children, *Highlights of Official Child Neglect and Abuse Reporting, 1986* (Denver: American Humane Association, 1987).

9. R. Blum and C. Runyan, "Adolescent Abuse: The Dimensions of the Problem" *Journal of Adolescent Health Care* 1 (1980):121–26.

10. J. Powers and J. Eckenrode, "The Maltreatment of Adolescents," *Child Abuse and Neglect* 12 (1988):189–99.

11. See Fisher and Berdie, "Adolescent Abuse and Neglect;" J. Garbarino, C. Schellenbach, and J. Sebes, eds. *Troubled Youth, Troubled Families* (New York: Aldine Publishers, 1986).

12. Garbarino, Schellenbach, and Sebes, *Troubled Youth.*

13. Ira Lourie, "Family Dynamics and the Abuse of Adolescents: A Case for a Developmental Phase Specific Model of Child Abuse," *Child Abuse and Neglect* 3 (1979) 967–74.

14. Fisher et al., *Adolescent Abuse and Neglect.*

15. Berdie and Wexler, "Preliminary Research."

16. See Garbarino, Schellenbach, and Sebes, *Troubled Youth;* Berdie and Wexler, "Preliminary Research;" E. Farber and J. Joseph, "The Maltreated Adolescent: Patterns of Physical Abuse," *Child Abuse and Neglect* 9 (1985):201–6.

17. Fisher and Berdie, "Adolescent Abuse and Neglect."

18. Berdie and Wexler, "Preliminary Research."

19. Gaye Moorehead, (Rochester, N.Y.: Society for the Prevention of Cruelty to Children), lectures and presentations for STAR Project Training, Spring 1986.

20. Suzanne Sgroi, *Handbook of Clinical Intervention in Child Sexual Abuse* (Lexington, Mass.: Lexington Books, 1982).

21. Lourie, "Family Dynamics and the Abuse of Adolescents."

22. Ibid.

23. Ibid., 967.

Chapter 3. Psychological and Behavioral Effects of Maltreatment

1. Claudia Jewett, *Helping Children Cope with Separation and Loss* (Harvard, Mass.: Harvard Common Press, 1982).

2. E. Farber and J. Joseph, "The Maltreated Adolescent: Patterns of Physical Abuse," *Child Abuse and Neglect* 9 (1985): 201–6.

3. B. Fisher, J. Berdie, J. Cook, and N. Day, *Adolescent Abuse and Neglect: Intervention Strategies* (Washington, D.C.: DHHS Publication No. [OHDS] 80-30266, 1980).

4. See A. Browne and D. Finkelhor, "Impact of Child Sexual Abuse: A Review of the Research," *Psychological Bulletin* 99 (1986): 66–77.

5. P. Moran and J. Eckenrode, "Personality Variables Related to Depression in Maltreated Adolescent Females" (Paper presented at the Second Family Violence Research Conference, Durham, NH, 1987).

6. E. Gil, *Outgrowing the Pain* (San Francisco: Launch Press, 1983): 32.

7. B. Jaklitsch and M. Beyer, *Preparing for Independence: Counseling Issues with the Maltreated Adolescent* (Norman: University of Oklahoma, National Resource Center for Youth Services, in press).

8. Gil, *Outgrowing the Pain,* 58.

9. Ibid., 29

10. M. Beyer, "Overcoming Emotional Obstacles to Independence," *Children and Youth Today* (Sept.–Oct. 1986): 8–12.

11. Gil, *Outgrowing the Pain,* 18–19.

12. Jaklitsch and Beyer, *Preparing for Independence.*

13. Linda Sanford, "Pervasive Fears of Victims in Sexual Abuse: A Clinician's Observations," *Preventing Sexual Abuse* (Newsletter of the National Family Life Education Network) 2:2 (1987).

14. See, A. Groth, W. Hobson, & T. Gary, "The child molester: Clinical observation." In S.B. Smith, *Children's Story: Children in Criminal Court.* Sacramento, CA: California District Attorney's Office (1985) and F. Knopp, The Youthful Sex Offender: The Rationale and Goals of Early Intervention and Treatment. Syracuse, N.Y.: Safer Society Press (1985), cited in D. Edwards and E. Gil, *Breaking the Cycle: Assessment and Treatment of Child Abuse and Neglect* (Los Angeles: Association for Advanced Training in the Behavioral Sciences, 1985).

15. See D. Boyer and J. James "Easy Money: Adolescent Involvement in Prostitution" In K. Weisberg (ed.) *Women and the Law: The Interdisciplinary Perspective* (Cambridge: Schuckman, 1981), cited in R. Young, W. Godfrey, B. Mathews, and G. Adams, "Runaways: A Review of Negative Consequences," *Family Relations* 32 (1983): 275–81.

16. A. Goldstein and B. Glick, *Aggression Replacement Training: A Comprehensive Intervention* (Champaign, Ill.: Research Press, 1987).

17. Jewett, *Helping Children Cope.*

18. Jaklitsch and Beyer, *Preparing for Independence.*

19. See L. Anderson, "Notes on the Linkage between the Sexually Abused Child and the Suicidal Adolescent," *Journal of Adolescence* 4 (1981): 157–62; D. Shaffer and C. Caton, *Runaway and Homeless Youth in New York City: A Report to the Ittleson Foundation* (New York: Division of Child Psychiatry, New York State Psychiatric Institute and Columbia University College of Physicians and Surgeons, 1984).

20. M.J. Rotheram and J. Bradley, *Evaluation and Triage of Runaways at*

Risk for Suicide (New York: Division of Child Psychiatry, Columbia University, 1986).

21. Beyer, "Overcoming Emotional Obstacles."

22. Ibid.

Chapter 4. Interviewing and Disclosure

1. D. Edwards and E. Gil, *Breaking the Cycle: Assessment and Treatment of Child Abuse and Neglect* (Los Angeles: Association for Advanced Training in the Behavioral Sciences, 1985).

2. Linda Sanford, "Pervasive Fears of Victims in Sexual Abuse: A Clinician's Observations," *Preventing Sexual Abuse (Newsletter of the National Family Life Education Network)* 2:2 (1987).

Index

About the Authors

Jane Levine Powers received her Ph.D. in 1985 from the Department of Human Development and Family Studies, Cornell University, and her B.A. from the Residential College of the University of Michigan in 1977. Since 1985 she has been a research associate at Cornell's Family Life Development Center where she has worked on various projects involving child maltreatment.

She is currently developing a National Archive of research relevant to child abuse and neglect. She lives in Ithaca, New York, with her husband and two daughters.

Barbara Weiss Jaklitsch has been working with and on behalf of victimized youth since the early 1970s. She was the former training coordinator for Cornell University's STAR project, where she developed staff training materials on adolescent maltreatment and runaway and homeless youth. Prior to joining STAR she was Director of Family House, a program for homeless, runaway, and troubled young people. Her early experience was in the Washington, D.C. area where she did family, individual, and group counseling with at-risk youth and families, street outreach, and training.

Barbara is the author of *STAR Buddy Training System: Adolescent Abuse*. She has presented at conferences throughout the country on topics related to maltreated adolescents, runaway and homeless youth, and preparing youth in care for independence. She is currently a training specialist at Tabor Children's Services in Philadelphia. She lives outside Philadelphia with her husband and two daughters.